Exploring the Seashore
in British Columbia, Washington and Oregon

A Guide to Shorebirds and Intertidal Plants and Animals

Gloria Snively

Edited by Gordon R. Elliott

Gordon Soules Book Publishers Ltd.
West Vancouver, Canada
Seattle, U.S.A.

First printing, 1978
Second printing, 1979
Third printing, 1980
Fourth printing, 1981
Fifth printing, 1983
Sixth printing, 1985
Seventh printing, 1987
Eighth printing, 1989
Ninth printing, 1992

Canadian Cataloguing in Publication Data

Snively, Gloria, 1943–
    Exploring the Seashore in British Columbia,
    Washington and Oregon

    Bibliography: p.
    Includes index.
    ISBN 0-919574-25-4

1. Seashore biology—British Columbia
2. Seashore biology—Washington (State)
3. Seashore biology—Oregon. I. Title.
QH95.7.S55   574.971'1   C78-002187-8

Library of Congress Catalog Card Number: 78-63412

Published in Canada by
Gordon Soules Book Publishers Ltd.
1352-B Marine Drive
West Vancouver, B.C.
Canada   V7T 1B5

Published in the U.S.A. by
Gordon Soules Book Publishers Ltd.
620-1916 Pike Place
Seattle, WA 98101

Designed by Chris Bergthorson & Gloria Snively
Maps by Michael John Winfield
Typeset by Domino-Link Word & Data Processing Ltd.
Printed and bound in Canada by Hignell Printing Limited.

Table Of Contents

Acknowledgements

Any person growing up on our coast should be able to recall many happy visits to the seashore, should remember seeing the Purple Sea Stars, the Green Sea Urchins, the low-rolling fog, and the brilliant sunsets; should remember hearing the waves crashing to shore, the seagulls crying, and the foghorns in the distance; and remember walking barefoot on the cold wet sand and touching the white foam cast ashore during winter storms.

Though I remember such explorations clearly and fondly, the seashore was unfortunately never really a part of my formal education. In fact, not until I had been graduated from university and had become an elementary school teacher did I have a basic two-week course on intertidal life given for non-biology students at Cannon Beach, Oregon. Professor Ruth Winchell of the University of Oregon was the instructor who made the study of sea life both intriguing and exciting. And she had the patience to teach me to explore, to observe, and to question. While working on this book I gradually realized how many other people played a part in developing my marine interests. I realized, as well, that although I have learned a lot about the seashore I am still no real expert.

As an elementary school teacher I conducted many field trips to many types of beaches, and though I had considerable satisfaction from teaching the children, I was hardly able to answer their many questions: What's inside a barnacle? Why do hermit crabs live in snail shells? How does the starfish eat the clam? What's that called? Is that a plant or an animal? To save face I began a search of the literature, but to my dismay could find no single guide to the marine life of this area, at least no single guide that did not take for granted a good grounding in biology. For the next few years I simply did the best I could: set up classroom aquariums and took my classes to different beaches. For those happy years I am grateful to my students with their curiosity, their desire to learn, and their incessant questions. I appreciate, too, the dozens of faithful parents, such as Mr. Harold Stamnes, who accompanied us on those trips. And I am certainly indebted to Mr. Steve Cribb, my principal, for putting up with wet classroom floors and rancid smells that more than once permeated the entire building, and for trusting me to "bring all those kids back from the beach". After "making do" myself and after taking other enthusiastic, but bewildered teachers on field trips, I decided that a guide for beginners and newcomers was absolutely necessary.

I am extremely grateful to my teaching colleagues and to the professional biologists. Dr. Milton McClaren and Dr. Selma Wassermann, both of the Faculty of Education at Simon Fraser University, British Columbia, encouraged me to write this book and advised on the tentative framework for it. Dr. Eugene Kozloff of the Friday Harbor Research Station, Washington, and Dr. Tom Carefoot, marine biologist at the University of British Columbia, gave professional advice and read the manuscript for errors in biological fact. Jane Lamb, professor of marine biology at Portland Community College, Oregon, identified specimens, reviewed the manuscript, and examined the sketches for detail.

Acknowledgements

Others gave various kinds of specialized help. My brother John, professor of geology at Clackamas Community College, Oregon, taught me to notice the geology of beaches and he read the sections on types of coastlines. Terry Hood, a teaching colleague, and Kevin Bell, naturalist at the Lynn Canyon Ecology Centre, North Vancouver, took me on birdwatching expeditions and read the sections on shorebirds. Sandy Millen, Dr. Peter Fankboner, Dr. D.B. Quayle, and the staffs of the Vancouver Public Aquarium, the Pacific Environment Institute, and the Nanaimo Research Station, helped in identifying specimens and gave assistance in their own special fields.

In finding the artists I was extremely fortunate. Philip Croft's concern for accuracy, his life-long love of natural history, and his patience and endurance in completing the 230 sketches impressed me greatly; as did his wife Edith who supplied us constantly with cakes and cookies and tea. The bird sketches by the remarkably talented Mark Wynja also delighted me. John Snively, Terry Hood, and Neil Stainton contributed photographs of shorelines. Phil Edgell and Rick Harbo, two divers, produced several of the extraordinary underwater color photographs. However, Ron Long, photographer for biological sciences at Simon Fraser University, and Neil McDaniel, marine biologist at Pacific Environment Institute, West Vancouver, produced most of them and are now writing their own books. Ron and Neil also reviewed the manuscript, identified specimens, and examined the sketches for detail.

More thanks go to many friends with whom I shared the seashores: Nancy and Larry Burroughs, Sharie Conroy, Ed Dowling, Tamar Griggs, Ib Hansen, Brian Herrin, Ed Jackson, Stan and Margaret King, Jane Lamb, Milt McClaren, Arlene and Gordon McLaughlin, Charlie Metzger, Joan Mitchell, Kit Slade, John Snively, Harvey Walker, and Larry Wolfson. My thanks also go to Karen Davis who besides exploring the beach helped with the enormous task of typing the manuscript. And to Linda Jacobson, Maureen O'Sullivan, Peggy Reed, and June Wyatt for constant and continued listening and laughing.

I also thank those people who helped produce this book. To Gordon Elliott, professor of English at Simon Fraser University, for creative editing, and for teaching me so much about the English language. To Barbara Tomlin and Margaret Campbell for a superb job of proofing the galleys. To Chris Bergthorson and Ben Lim for patient help and advice in layout technicalities. And to Gordon Soules for being the special kind of publisher that he just happens to be.

Acknowledgements

ART CREDITS
Intertidal plants and animals by Philip Croft
Shorebirds by Mark Wynja

PHOTOGRAPHIC CREDITS — numbers refer to plates
Phil Edgell
10, 45, 80, 81, 82, 94
Frank Grundig
front cover, 113, 118, back cover
Rick Harbo
22, 28, 30, 41, 43, 49, 62, 74, 84, 91, 93
Terry Hood
101, 102
Ron Long
2, 8, 12, 13, 14, 15, 16, 17, 19, 20, 23, 24, 25, 27, 29, 31, 33, 35, 36, 37, 38, 42, 48, 51, 65, 79, 92
Neil McDaniel
1, 3, 4, 5, 6, 7, 9, 11, 18, 21, 26, 32, 34, 39, 40, 44, 46, 47, 50, 52, 54, 55, 56, 57, 58, 59, 60, 61, 63, 64, 66, 67, 68, 69, 70, 71, 72, 73, 75, 76, 77, 78, 83, 85, 86, 87, 89, 90
Russ Simpson
53
Gloria Snively
88, 96, 97, 98, 100, 103, 104, 105, 106, 109, 110, 112, 114, 116
John Snively
95, 99, 107, 108, 111, 117
Neil Stainton
115

This is a book for people who want to know more about the seashore, more about the plants and animals than just their names. It is a book for the genuinely curious, for people who want to understand life on our seashores and want to understand why certain plants and animals live where they live, eat what they eat, behave as they do behave, and protect themselves in the ways they do protect themselves.

This guide includes the common and some of the not-so-common intertidal plants and animals that inhabit our shores and a few of the hungry shorebirds which emphasize the twice-daily changing of the tides, and dramatize the conflict between predator and prey. It simplifies identification of these plants and animals by arranging them according to the type of beach, the tidal zone, and the habitat in which they normally live. Take, for example, plants and animals which live on rocky shores. Some live higher up on the beach, others live lower down; some live on the top of rocks, and some live under them; still others live in tidepools or in burrows dug in sand or mud: habitat determines, in part, the kinds and numbers living there. Go to a particular type of beach — rock, sand, cobble, or mud. Match the place on the beach where you locate an organism — on rocks, under rocks, or in tidepools — with the band at the top of the page. And use the index to locate organisms not easily grouped according to habitat.

Call the creatures what you like, even "bugs", or "beasties", or "critters", this guide stresses understanding how they are equipped to live in their world. Such an understanding brings an appreciation for conservation and suggests leaving the specimens where you found them. Enjoy your experience at the seashore. Learn the scientific names if you wish. Come to appreciate the delicate balance of life between the tides. But most important, understand why and how these plants and animals live on the beach, and understand the interrelationships between them and the environment in which they live.

Identifying the Type of Beach

A Rocky Shore

Rocky shore plants and animals have special attaching devices to allow for holding onto rocks in strong waves and many animals make their homes here under the rocks or among the thick growths of seaweeds protecting them from waves and from drying out. The dropping tide level often leaves interesting tidepools. Generally speaking, the rocky shore is a stable home, and because it is stable it is home to a great diversity and abundance of species.

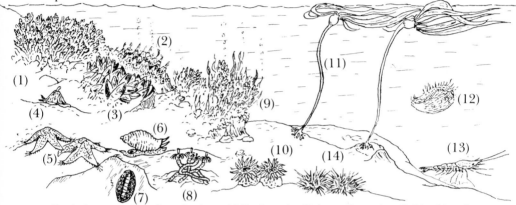

Vertical cross-section of a rocky shore. (1) Rockweeds; (2) Acorn Barnacles; (3) Blue Mussels; (4) Keyhole Limpet; (5) Purple or Ochre Sea Stars; (6) Rock Whelk; (7) Black Chiton; (8) Calcareous Tube Worms; (9) Rockweed; (10) Giant Green Sea Anemones; (11) Bull Kelp; (12) Pink Scallop; (13) Coon-striped Shrimp; (14) Red Sea Urchins.

A Sandy Beach

On sandy beaches of the outer coast the constant movement of sand creates an unstable and therefore unfavorable habitat. Animals on exposed sandy beaches must, therefore, protect themselves: some dig or burrow into the sand, and most, such as shrimp, are free-moving and able to re-establish themselves when the sand stops shifting. Sandy beaches in protected areas become mixed with fine mud and have a greater variety and number of plants and animals than exposed beaches. On some protected sandy beaches eelgrass beds stabilize the bottom, the roots, stipes, and blades providing shelter to a wide variety of small animals.

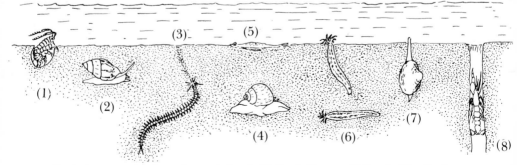

Vertical cross-section through a sandy beach. (1) Beach Hopper; (2) Purple Olive Snail; (3) Sand Worm; (4) Moon Snail; (5) Sand Sole; (6) Burrowing Sea Cucumber; (7) Sand Clam; (8) Ghost Shrimp.

A Mud Flat

Mud mixes with sands, gravels, and varying amounts of water so that some mud beaches are firm enough to walk on, while others are soupy. Mud flats form only in the most protected bays and estuaries where fine sediments have settled, and often contain decomposing plant and animal matter, as well as bacteria, to serve as food for many organisms. Mud flats have few hard surfaces for attachment, and the problems of moving, food gathering, and breathing are great. Thus, most animals live either near the surface or in tubes or shallow burrows open to it.

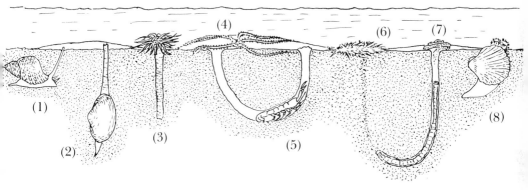

Vertical cross-section through a mud flat. (1) Black Dog Whelk; (2) Mud Clam; (3) Tube-dwelling Anemone; (4) Brittle Star; (5) Mud Shrimp; (6) Sea Mouse; (7) Lugworm; (8) Cockle Clam.

A Cobblestone Beach

A cobblestone beach sheltered from strong wave action provides a mixture of cobbles, gravel, sand and mud. Certain animals here can burrow readily: clams and worms. There is an abundance of seaweeds, but as they become larger and more buoyant some float away, dragging their little rock anchors with them. Animals here generally live "in" the beach rather than on it.

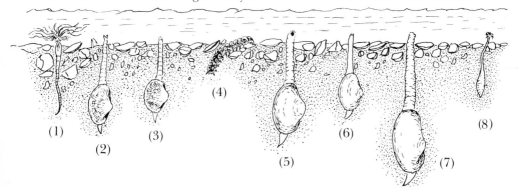

Vertical cross-section through a cobblestone beach. (1) Hairy Gilled Worm; (2) Japanese Little-neck Clam; (3) Native Little-neck Clam; (4) Armored Scaleworm; (5) Horse Clam; (6) Butter Clam; (7) Geoduck Clam; (8) Peanut Worm.

Identifying Tidal Zones On A Beach

Twice each day the tide rises and falls. Twice each day the seashore is either covered with sea water or exposed to air or rain, and sometimes to the drying effect of the sun. Beaches are divided into zones or areas according to the length of time they are covered by water or exposed to air.

The Spray Zone

First and highest is the upper beach, or Spray Zone, an area flooded only by the highest storm waves and the ocean spray, and almost completely dry much of the time. During periods of heavy rain, though, animals here must tolerate rapid changes in the salt content of the water. They must also be able to retain moisture for long periods and must be able to withstand both freezing cold and extreme heat.

The High Tide Zone

Just below the Spray Zone, the High Tide Zone is an area normally uncovered except during high tides, and the home of animals more conditioned to air than to water. This area, too, has many changes of temperature, water cover, and salt content. When the tide is in, the organisms are affected by moving currents, and many depend on the tides and waves to carry food.

The Middle Tide Zone

The Middle Tide Zone is typically covered and uncovered twice each day and the great numbers of animals here may require the rise and fall of the tides. Temperature changes are less, because the Middle Tide Zone is covered with water much of the time.

The Low Tide Zone

The Low Tide Zone is always covered except during the•very lowest tides. A more constant area, having fewer changes in temperature, exposure, or salt content, it supports subtidal animals that move up as far as possible from deep water. Most animals here are unable to exist any higher up than this zone. A very crowded area, it has more plants and animals than all the other tidal zones combined.

Identifying Tidal Zones On A Beach

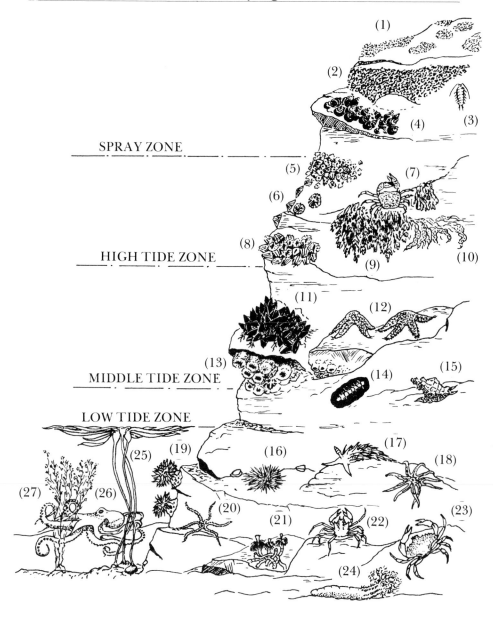

SPRAY ZONE

HIGH TIDE ZONE

MIDDLE TIDE ZONE

LOW TIDE ZONE

Cross-section showing vertical zonation on a rocky shore. (1) Lichens; (2) Blue-green Algae; (3) Rock Louse; (4) Periwinkles; (5) Small Acorn Barnacles; (6) Finger Limpets; (7) Rock Crab; (8) Common Acorn Barnacles; (9) Rockweed; (10) Sea Lettuce; (11) Blue Mussels; (12) Purple or Ochre Sea Stars; (13) Aggregate Anemones; (14) Black Chiton; (15) Wrinkled Whelk; (16) Red Sea Urchin; (17) Opalescent Nudibranch; (18) Sun Star; (19) Giant Green Sea Anemone; (20) Brittle Star; (21) Calcareous Tube Worm; (22) Kelp Crab; (23) Red Rock Crab; (24) Orange Sea Cucumber; (25) Bull Kelp; (26) Octopus; (27) Sargassum.

Identifying Habitats On A Beach

The habitat of a plant or an animal is its natural home and this book groups plants and animals according to the habitat in which they are most frequently found.

On Rocks

Plants and animals living on rocks must have specialized methods of attaching themselves to those rocks. Some seaweeds, for example, have tangled root-like structures called holdfasts, while barnacles cement themselves to rocks, and mussels anchor themselves with long, elastic threads.

In Crevices

The cracks, crevices, and holes on rocks provide shaded and moist retreats from the hot sun for some animals, for snails, limpets, and small crabs. Some crevices hold water, and thus enable the plants and animals to survive higher on the beach than they would normally.

Under Rocks

The under-rock habitat is continuously moist and plants and animals living there cannot survive long in the sun. The crabs, brittle stars, blennies, and clingfish hide under the rocks at low tide and tube worms adhere to the undersides of the same rocks.

Among Seaweeds

The holdfasts, stipes, and fronds of seaweeds provide food and shelter for a host of animals, especially those without protective shells, such as nudibranchs, or "sea slugs". Some seaweeds, such as rockweeds and eelgrass, act as a nursery for small snails and limpets, while shrimps, crabs, amphipods, isopods, and worms cling to the stems, fronds, and holdfasts of kelps.

In Tidepools

A tidepool is a small pool of water left on a rocky shore when the tide falls and provides shelter for plants and animals that cannot stand exposure to air during low tide periods. Some pools are so small, however, that they may be warmed by the sun and therefore may have a low dissolved oxygen content and salt content higher than that of the sea. Every tidepool contains a community of plants and animals: some are bottom dwellers; some attach themselves to the sides; others are free-swimming.

In Surface Sand

Animals living at the surface of sand must be able to move freely as the sand moves and then re-establish themselves when the sand stops moving. Several species of little amphipods, isopods, shrimp and fish live at the surface and may become temporarily dislodged when water sloshes over them. In quiet-water beaches there will also be a variety of worms which feed on the diatoms and particles of decomposed plant and animal matter at the surface.

In Surface Mud

Because mud does not allow for the free movement of oxygen, only the top few centimeters will contain a great assortment of organisms — diatoms, amphipods, and isopods; tiny worms, clams, and shrimp. A variety of larger worms crowd at the surface unless forced to retreat by bright sunlight: nemerteans, flatworms, and segmented worms.

Burrowing In Mixed Cobble, Gravel, Sand, And Mud

Few plants and animals can survive the tumbling action of the constantly moving gravel beaches on the open coast, but in protected waters, where there is little wave action, gravel mixes with sand, broken shell, cobbles, or mud and provides a loose bottom on which burrowing animals can burrow easily. This is the home of clams with their comparatively thick, protective shells, and of an assortment of burrowing worms.

Burrowing In Sand

Although most sand flat animals burrow somewhat, the few strictly burrowing forms must be able to dig rapidly or must have heavy shells to protect them from the harsh abrasive action of moving sand — the notoriously fast Razor Clam of the outer coast and the thick shelled Sand Clam on more protected beaches.

Burrowing In Mud

Because mud does not allow free movement of oxygen, very specialized animals live either in tubes or in burrows open to the surface. Mud burrowing clams have soft and fragile shells and siphons open to the surface for food and oxygen.

Burrowing In Soft Rock

Regions of stiff clay, hard mud, or soft rock support an extremely limited but highly specialized group of boring clams. The rough Piddock Clam has an extremely long siphon, has grinding "teeth" on the shell, and lives in a permanent burrow in exposed rocky reefs, as well as in hard clay.

Burrowing In Wood

Above the high tide line on almost any beach, old logs, planks, and pieces of driftwood have been stranded by high tides and storm waves. Many pieces have been riddled with countless holes, or burrows, either by wood boring clams called "shipworms", or by wood boring isopods called "gribbles".

Some Final Words About Using This Field Guide

Arranging plants and animals according to habitat, tidal zone, and the type of shore enables the matching of an organism in the guide with the place where it was found on the beach. But such a method of organization has its own problems.

As the tide ebbs over a beach, the animals not attached to hard surfaces must find suitable places to hide from the drying sun and from new predators such as hungry shorebirds. Some intertidal animals, and many crabs and snails are extremely hardy and not too particular about where they hide. As the water drops they may slide under moist rocks or into crevices, or simply become stranded on a rock or in a tidepool, but most plants and animals require more specific conditions for their survival and live in specific habitats.

That zones occur is obvious, but like everything else in nature, zones are not simple patterns. On a seashore they may vary with the tidal cycles, the speed of currents, and the degree of exposure to waves, all themselves determined by such factors as whether or not the shore is protected or exposed. Zones may also vary according to the climate and according to the season; for example, certain seaweeds live their entire lives in one growing season and die off in winter. Zones on a vertical rock face are close together and appear as distinct, horizontal bands, but on a rocky shore with a gentle slope the zones spread out and overlap. Nevertheless, the zones on a rocky shore look pretty much the same in England, Australia, South Africa, the United States, and Canada. When identifying zones on a beach, look for indicator seaweeds and for indicator animals such as barnacles because these organisms are permanently attached to hard surfaces. Organisms such as crabs and sea stars are not attached and some species are capable of wide-ranging movement.

Protect Seashore Plants And Animals

The plants and animals in the intertidal regions of the seashore are specially equipped to live in particular habitats and each group of organisms depends upon other groups for food. Thus the plants and animals living in a particular area depend on each other for survival. If unthinking visitors start turning over rocks, digging up the sand and mud, and carting animals away to die in buckets or to suffocate in poorly prepared aquariums, the area would require a long time to recover. One can, however, visit the seashore and cause very little damage, but only by understanding the plants and animals and their habitats. Investigate the plants and animals and their habitats; investigate them and enjoy them, but do not destroy them.

Turn The Rocks Back Over

When turning over a rock, do so gently. Try not to crush too many animals living on, beside, or under the rock. Put the rock back the way it was, or lean it face down against another rock.

Fill In Any Holes

When digging for burrowing animals do not leave piles of sand or mud on the beach: many burrowing animals float away or die when the tide returns. Furthermore, the unnatural holes, and piles of mud or sand may kill many small clams or other animals whose burrows can no longer reach the surface.

Cover Abandoned Animals With Seaweed

When investigating animals living on or under seaweeds return the animals and cover them again with moist protective weed, otherwise the sun may dry them out.

Avoid Walking On Animals

When walking on rocky shores try to walk on bare rocks or on the patches of sand and mud between rocks. Try not to crush barnacles and other organisms living on the surface. Do not run.

Leave The Specimens In Their Natural Habitat

Do all of your investigating at the seashore. Do not move animals from one tidal zone or one type of beach to another. Do not take any organisms away.

Do Not Mount, Dry, or Preserve Specimens

Many people boil snails to make jewelry from the beautiful shells, or dry sea stars and sea urchins to decorate basements and bulletin boards. For such purposes use only the discarded shells of animals already dead.

Follow The Legal Regulations

Check and abide by the local fish, crab, and shellfish regulations on the legal size and limits set for individual species.

Camp And Leave No Trace

Put out any fire you might build and scatter the pieces. Pack out all of your garbage. In every way, try to leave the beach and its inhabitants as they were.

Rules For Safety

Know The Area

Before planning a trip to the seashore gather as much information about it as possible. Go to the safe protected bays, inlets, and estuaries. Avoid cliffs, caves, and sandbars.

Learn "Indicator Organisms"

Plants and animals live in particular habitats. Some organisms, such as the Purple Sea Urchin, Goose Neck Barnacle, California Blue Mussel, and Sea Palm are especially suited for living in the violent surf-swept world of exposed shores. Avoid shores with these organisms.

Check The Tides

Learn to read a tide table. Before going to the beach know how low the tide will fall and at what time the tide will start to rise.

Keep Your Eye On The Ocean

Continually check your times and locations. People often become so involved with looking at tidepools that the rising tide cuts them off from the land and they become stranded. Do not keep your back to the sea.

Know Your Waves

Every seventh wave is not higher and those in between are not safer: sometimes several high waves follow in succession. Never turn your back to the sea until you are familiar with the wave action of the area.

If Caught In A Wave

If caught by an unexpected wave, don't run. Lie down, like a barnacle or a sea star, and cling tightly to the rocks. Let the water pour over you.

Motor Boats

Take care when a ferry or speed boat comes near: the huge waves can sweep you away.

Wear A Life Jacket

Avoid exploring near deep water that is over your head. Always wear a life jacket when exploring close to deep water and when out in boats.

Do Not Climb Shoreline Rock Faces

Do not climb cliffs facing the ocean: the tide will rise and might trap you. In addition, shoreline cliffs are frequently of soft sandstone or clay, and might crumble beneath your weight.

Never Walk On Floating Logs

Do not walk on log booms or on stranded logs in shallow water. Loose floating logs roll unpredictably. Avoid walking on logs resting on beaches in bays and along estuaries: an incoming tide can turn them over or sweep them away.

Never Fool Around

Don't play practical jokes. Do not run or push or shove. Such fun might end in tragedy.

Explore In Groups

Never explore alone. Always explore with a partner and preferably in threes — if one is hurt the second can stay while the third goes for help.

1 A Giant Acorn Barnacle, *Balanus nubilus*, with its feathery appendages, p. 121

2 Hairy Hermit Crab, *Pagurus hirsutiusculus,* p. 78

3 Purple Shore Crab, *Hemigrapsus nudus,* p. 81

4 Juvenile Puget Sound King Crab, *Lopholithodes mandtii,* p. 141

5 Oregon Rock Crab, *Cancer oregonensis,* p. 140

6 Dungeness Crab, *Cancer magister,* p. 164

7 Red Rock Crab, *Cancer productus,* p. 139

8 A Decorator Crab, *Oregonia gracilis,* camouflaged with white bryozoans, p. 126

9 A Sharp-nosed Crab, *Scyra acutifrons,* masked with sponges, bryozoans,
and seaweeds, p. 127

19

10 The Mud Shrimp, *Upogebia pugettensis*, p. 189

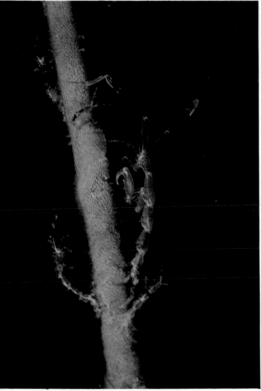

11 Skeleton Shrimps, *Caprella* sp., clinging to kelp, p. 159

12 One of the numerous species of Kelp Fleas, Amphipods, p. 79

13 Spindle Whelk, *Searlesia dira,* p. 95

14 Wrinkled Whelk, *Thais lamellosa,* p. 95

15 Wrinkled Amphissa, *Amphissa columbiana,* p. 115

16 Purple Olive, *Olivella biplicata,* p. 157

17 Opalescent Top Shell, *Calliostoma annulatum,* p. 115

18 Blue Top Shell, *Calliostoma ligatum,* p. 114

19 Leafy Hornmouth, *Ceratostoma foliatum,* p. 118

20 White Cap Limpet, *Acmaea mitra,* p. 121, covered with pink Rock Crust

21

21 Wrinkled Whelks, *Thais lamellosa,* with their stalked egg cases, called "sea oats", p. 95

22 Clusters of Oregon Hairy Triton egg capsules, *Fusitriton oregonensis,* p. 118

23 Moon Snail, *Polinices lewisii*, with its enormous fleshy foot extended, p. 156

24 Northern Abalone, *Haliotis kamtschatkana*, with its tentacles and foot extended, p. 119

25 A Heart Cockle, *Clinocardium nuttallii*, its short siphons filtering plankton, p. 186

26 Pink Scallops, *Chlamys hericia*, looking like false teeth on the rocky bottom and covered with a sponge coating for protection from predatory sea stars, p. 122

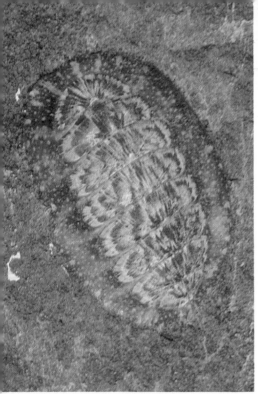

27 Hairy Chiton, *Mopalia lignosa*, p. 112

28 Black Chiton, *Katharina tunicata*, p. 87

29 Lined Chiton, *Tonicella lineata*, p. 113

30 Gum Boot Chiton, *Cryptochiton stelleri*, p. 113

31 Frosted Nudibranch, *Dirona albolineata,* p. 128

32 Sea Lemon, *Archidoris montereyensis,* p. 129

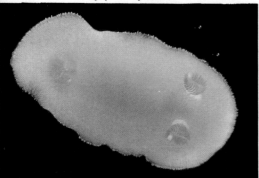

33 Shaggy Mouse Nudibranch, *Aeolidea papillosa,* p. 161

34 Opalescent Nudibranch, *Hermissenda crassicornis,* p. 128

35 Red Nudibranch, *Rostanga pulchra,* p. 131

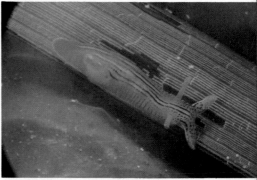

36 Green Sea Slug, *Phyllaplysia taylori,* p. 161

37 Ringed Nudibranch, *Diaulula sandiegensis,* p. 130

38 Yellow-edged Nudibranch, *Cadlina luteomarginata,* p. 130

39 The brilliant Orange-spotted Nudibranch, *Triopha carpenteri*, p. 130

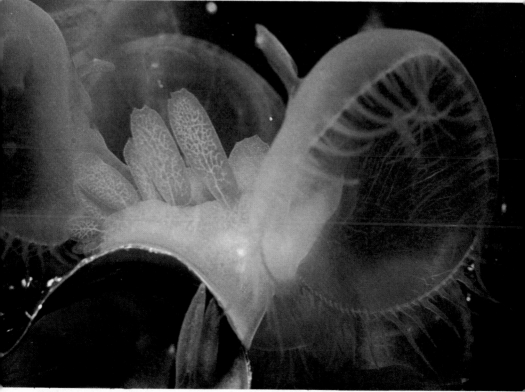

40 The transparent Hooded Nudibranch, *Melibe leonina*, captures prey with its specialized hood, p. 161

41 Eggs of the White Nudibranch, *Adalaria* sp., in a gelatinous ribbon on the protected sides of rocks, p. 129

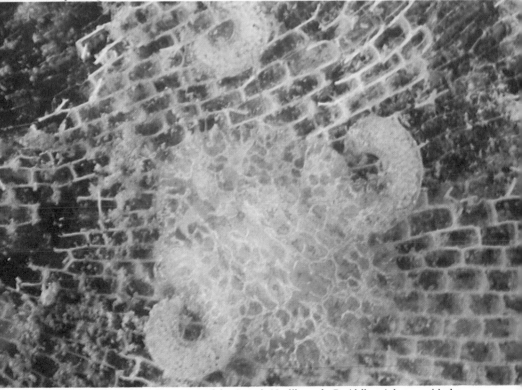

42 The crescent-shaped egg cases of the Cryptic Nudibranch, *Doridella steinbergae*, with the box-like houses of bryozoans on which it lives and feeds, p. 131

43 The Sunflower Star, *Pycnopodia helianthoides*, feeding on a mass of Ling Cod eggs, p. 108

44 Sun Star, *Solaster stimpsoni*, p. 108

45 Vermilion Star, *Mediaster aequalis*, p. 109

46 Daisy Brittle Star, *Ophiopholis aculeata*, on an Encrusting Sponge, p. 142

47 A Pink Star, *Pisaster brevispinus*, feeding on a clam, p. 107

48 Mottled Star, *Evasterias troschelii*, p. 106

49 Leather Star, *Dermasterias imbricata*, p. 106

50 Rose Star, *Crossaster papposus*, p. 109

51 Blood Star, *Henricia leviuscula*, p. 109

52 Six-rayed Star, *Leptasterias hexactis*, p. 107, attacking a Lined Chiton

53 Common Purple or Ochre Star, *Pisaster ochraceus*, feeding on a clam, p. 85

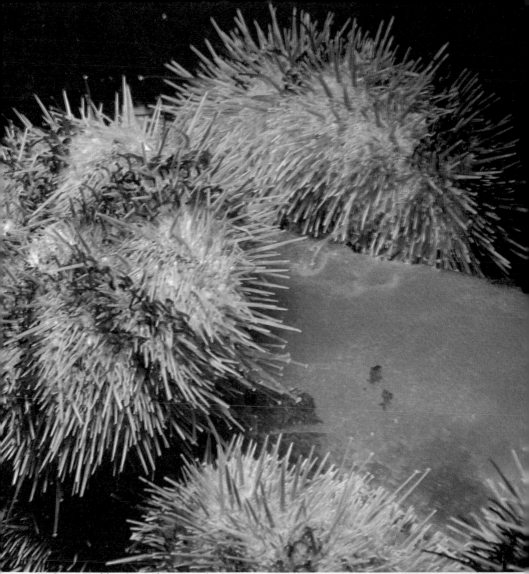

54 Green Urchins, *Strongylocentrotus droebachiensis*, grazing on kelp, p. 134

55 The surf-loving Purple Urchin,
Strongylocentrotus purpuratus, p. 135

56 The bristling Red Urchin,
Strongylocentrotus franciscanus, p. 134

57 Armored Sea Cucumber, *Psolus chitonoides*, with its bright red feeding tentacles, p. 139

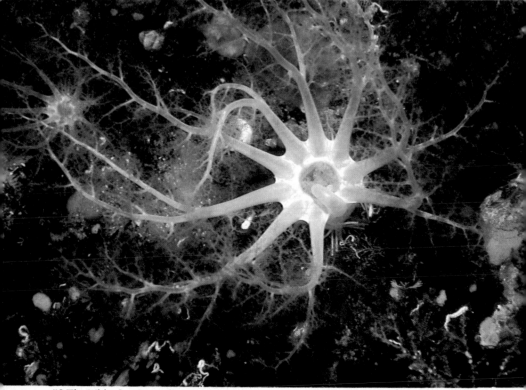

58 The White Sea Cucumber, *Eupentacta quinquesemita*, showing the feeding tentacles and the small circular mouth, p. 138

59 The California Sea Cucumber, *Parastichopus californicus*, arching its body and revealing its tube feet and mop-like tentacles, p. 185

60 Stalked Sea Squirt, *Styela montereyensis,* p. 110

61 Hairy Sea Squirt, *Boltenia villosa,* p. 183

62 Red Sea Squirt, *Cnemidocarpa finmarkiensis,* p. 111

63 Sea Pork, *Aplidium californicum,* p. 111

64 The delicate Ostrich Plume Hydroid, *Aglaophenia struthionides,* p. 125

65 The mouth and transparent tentacles of Cup Corals, *Balanophyllia elegans,* p. 124

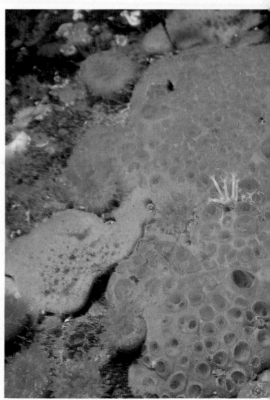

66 Solitary Cup Corals and a carpet of Encrusting Sponge, Phylum Porifera, p. 124

67 The waving and poisonous net of transparent tentacles of the Tube-dwelling Anemone, *Pachycerianthus fimbriatus*, p. 188

68 The Red and Green Anemone, *Tealia crassicornis*, expands to show its innocent flower-like posture. . .

69 . . .then paralyzes and digests an unsuspecting Green Urchin, p. 132

39

70 The Red-beaded Anemone, *Tealia coriacea*, burows into gravel and mud, p. 195

71 Clustering Aggregate Anemones, *Anthopleura elegantissima*, with pink-tipped tentacles, p. 87

72 A submerged cluster of feathery Plumose
Anemones, *Metridium senile*, p. 133

73 A Giant Green Anemone, *Anthopleura
xanthogrammica*, covered with broken
shell, p. 132

74 Brooding Anemone, *Epiactis prolifera*,
with young attached to the base
of the parent column, p. 133

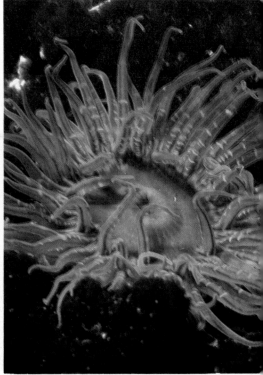

75 A Green Burrowing Anemone,
Anthopleura artemisia, lives in mud
or gravel, p. 195

76 A carnivorous Sea Pen, *Ptilosarcus gurneyi*, p. 168

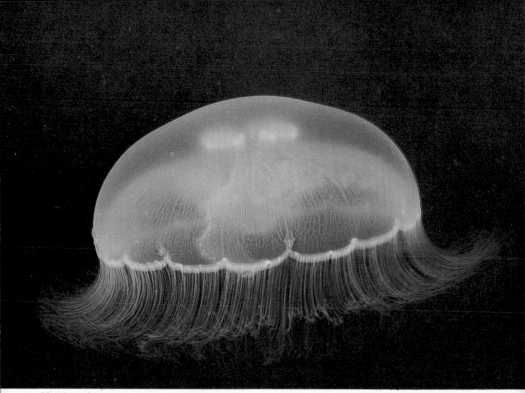

77 The softly shining Moon Jellyfish, *Aurelia aurita,* with its fringe of short tentacles, p. 152

78 The hundreds of tentacles of the Sea Nettle, *Cyanea capillata,* p. 152

79 A Stalked Jellyfish, *Haliclystus auricula,* attached to eelgrass, p. 162

80 A well-camouflaged Tidepool Sculpin, *Oligocottus maculosus,* p. 79

81 A Sand Sole, *Psettichthys melanosticus,* looking in two directions at once, p. 163

82 The Penpoint Gunnel, *Apodichthys flavidus*, p. 163, often mistaken for an eel, with a closed Giant Green Anemone

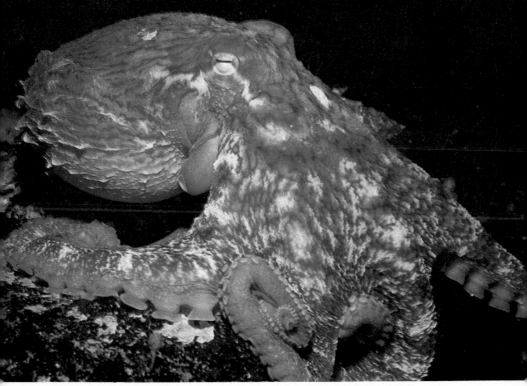

83 The Pacific Octopus, *Octopus dofleini*, capable of changing color: brown, black, gray, yellow, or red, p. 135

84 Rockweed, *Fucus* sp., p. 74, and Giant Green Anemones

85 Sea Moss, *Endocladia muricata*, p. 75

86 Graceful Coral Seaweed, *Corallina vancouveriensis*, p. 93

87 Coral Leaf Seaweed, *Bossiella* sp., p. 93

88 Sea Lettuce, *Ulva*, p. 74

89 Sea Sac, *Halosaccion glandiforme*, p. 89

90 Sea Hair, *Enteromorpha* sp., hanging
from rocks, p. 67

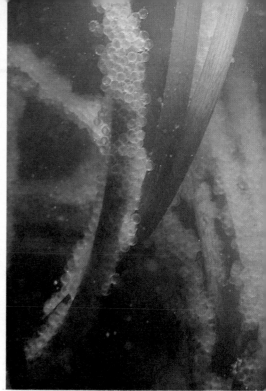

91 Herring eggs on Eelgrass,
Zostera marina, p. 158

92 Sea Palm, *Postelsia palmaeformis:*
a sure sign of violent surf, p. 89

93 An offshore forest of Bull Kelp,
Nereocystis luetkeana, p. 102

94 The rambling tubes and bright red tentacles of the Calcareous Tube Worm, *Serpula vermicularis*, p. 136

95 Arching white waves advancing against a rocky shore at Ecola State Park, Ore.

The Rocky Shore

A typical approach to a rocky shore is by a rough, winding path through an evergreen forest of hemlock, cedar, spruce, and fir — a low tide on a chilly, wet morning. Rolling fog drifting in and silently filling the forest. Among the living trees, many dead, ghostlike figures, blackened by fire. All the trees, the living and the dead, covered with mosses of various shades ranging from dark greens to pale yellows. Every branch of every tree draped with long tufts of coarse gray lichens called goat's beard. Here, in the dark shadows of the towering trees, whole armies of sword ferns, bracken ferns, and lady's fern. Here, also, tall bushes of Rose Bay, a shrub of the Rhododendron group, with its pale pink and rose-colored flowers, brighten the darkness. Lining the path on both sides are wild, edible berries: thimble berries, salmon berries, elder berries, and huckleberries. Wild ginger, lichens, and moss carpet the soggy wet ground.

Now the path winds to the edge of the forest where the darkness lightens into the pale, subdued colors of the open water. The offshore view is spectacular. A wild and beautiful coastline of jagged rocks, haystacks, arches, and rocky islands, all reminders of the relentless battle between the land and the sea: during storms and high tides, waves smash against the cliffs, eroding them with thousands of pounds of pressure; as the years pass the cliffs retreat and the shore pushes steadily inward.

Above Beach

On the coastal bluffs at the edge of the forest stand sturdy beach pines, their gnarled trunks and twisted branches indicating a slow growth on a harsh, wind-swept cliff. Interspersed with the pines, a crowd of coastal shrubs, the lot of them neatly trimmed and sculptured by coastal winds. One of these shrubs, Ceanothus, is like the small trees in a Japanese garden, but has tiny clusters of soft blue flowers. Another, Salal, spreads its shining leaves and dark purple fruit like a trimmed mat covering the ground. Solitary growths of Ocean Spray grow where there is neither full shade nor full sunlight, the rather large panicles of whitish flowers appearing from a distance to be soft ripples of ocean foam. Whole meadows of Indian Paint Brush brighten the clifftops with reds, oranges, and pinks. Fleshy leafed succulents of the stonecrop family maintain a precarious existence all along the bluffs and down over the faces where little or no plant life can sustain a foothold. Most obvious are the sedums which find nourishment in the tiny pockets of soil accumulated in the cracks and crevices.

The barren area below the top of the cliff harbors no plant life at all. Layer upon layer of sandstone, shale, and conglomerate lie exposed to erosion by wind and water and these marine sediments show that the sea level was once higher and that the ocean covered the land. Immediately below these layers is a great layer of dark volcanic basalt, a hard rock telling that molten lava once flowed into the sea, solidified and formed fragmented blocks. But the sea continued to wage war on the cliffs. Day by day, year by year, its attacks continued, taking advantage of every weakness, until it widened tiny holes, removed the fragments, and formed sea caves of considerable size and depth.

Framing the entrance to the cave and on a shelf above, clumps of pale violet daisies and yellow monkey flowers, their throats ornamented with tiny red specks. Inside, black lichens stain the walls everywhere. Fresh water seeps continuously down the sides. Water droplets, on the otherwise barren ceiling, one by one grow larger and heavier until they fall, each one in turn, making an echoing splash in the shallow pool of water entombed on the rock floor. The wreckage of the cliff piles up at the base of the cave. Larger stones are stranded at the entrance, but currents have carried the smaller pebbles out to sea, or sorted them according to size and deposited them at certain places on the beach.

The tide drops. Soon the rocks earlier concealed by high water glisten wet and various belts of colored seaweed appear in horizontal layers, one above the other. Bare rocks at the top, then a band of black lichens, then bright green seaweeds, luxuriant growths of browns, sometimes another layer of bright green and, on the lowest rocks, a band of reddish algae.

The dropping tide leaves glassy blue pools of water in holes or cracks. Clusters of white foam burst at the surface in the wake of the beating surf. Seaweeds of many colors line the walls and cast deep shadows: the vivid green strands of hair-like confetti, the heavy brown stems of kelp, the paper-thin blades of red laver. Attached to the rocks or moving freely about, whole cities of animals live in each tidepool, the collections differing depending on the location on the beach.

The rocky shore is home to the largest variety and the greatest number of seashore organisms. Animals occupy every available space: on rocks, under rocks, in crevices or holes, in tidepools, under the protective curtain of seaweeds, on the shells of other animals, and even in other plants and other animals themselves. Hordes of easily found rocky shore creatures, many brightly colored or of such bizarre shapes that they seem unreal: barnacles, limpets, chitons, snails, crabs, sea stars, sea anemones, sea urchins, worms, corals, and sponges.

With the ebbing of the tide comes a new drama: the gulls that earlier sat half asleep on the rocky crags stir to life and begin probing with their bills in the cracks, crevices, and seaweeds for small snails, crabs, and worms. Trying to distinguish one juvenile gull from another would result in confusion even for the seasoned bird watcher, because each species usually undergoes first, second, and third year plumage changes and the stages of several species closely resemble those of another.

Glaucous-winged Gull

The largest and most common is the Glaucous-winged Gull, *Larus glaucescens*, our only resident gull. The adults have clean, white heads, pale gray mantles, yellowish bills with a red spot, flesh colored legs, and strident voices. Like that of all gulls, the plumage of the young is variable. However, in all plumages, the wing tips are pale, not dark or black as in other gulls. The Glaucous-wing invades our cities and garbage dumps for food, and is the one most likely to steal the catches from diving ducks.

The gull most frequently competing with the Glaucous-wings for food in the winter is the Herring Gull, *Larus argentatus*, similar in size and appearance but with white-spotted, black-tipped wings. In England they follow the homeward-bound herring boats. One young Herring Gull pries a mussel loose, flies with it high into the air and brings forth squawks and screams from the other gulls. The circling gull lets the shellfish drop to smash the shell open on the hard basalt, and exposes the soft body inside. A new chorus of screams ensues, but before the Herring Gull can claim its meal an older Glaucous hurriedly snatches it up and with a mocking cry flies away with the loot.

Herring Gull

Flying low over the water, with feet dangling, and giving loud "mewing" calls comes the Mew Gull, *Larus canus*, a trim-looking gull, similar to the Herring Gull in color and form, but easier to identify because of its small height, up to 45 cm. In adults the head, neck, wings, and underparts are white; the mantle is bluish gray; the wing tips, black with white spots; the legs and short bill, greenish-yellow. Common along our coast during the fall, winter, and spring; in summer going to the northern breeding grounds. They frequently scavenge with larger gulls around garbage dumps, harbors, and sewage outlets, but are less aggressive and feed mainly on any available small fish.

Handsome, easily identified, Bonaparte's Gull, *Larus philadelphia*, is even smaller than the Mew Gull, up to 35 cm. In spring the distinctive solid black head, black-tipped white wings, and bright red legs separate the adults from other gulls, but in winter the black fades, leaving the head white with conspicuous dark ear patches. The Bonapartes are common transients during the fall and spring migration, but are rarely seen during the winter because they go south. In the fall they feed heavily on small fishes, such as herring and sandlance. Local fishermen often refer to the Bonapartes as "coho gulls" and by studying them frequently find schools of coho salmon which also feed on small fish.

Mew Gull

Boneparte's Gull

Bald Eagle

Common Murre

Over the barren rockface, a large and graceful bird soars boldly and without a sound, our largest bird of prey, the Bald Eagle, *Haliaeetus leucocephalus*. This giant with its white head, neck and tail rides the upcurrents and casts a shadow along the cliffs. Its presence makes the shorebirds below uneasy because the eagle can pick them off, not while they are on the wing but by attacking in the water. When given a choice, though, eagles feed on fish, preferably dead or dying. This once numerous species has been so persecuted by man that it has almost disappeared, and the coast of British Columbia and Alaska are its last strongholds.

Almost shoulder to shoulder among the highest rocks cluster the cliff-nesting Common Murres, *Uria aalge*, penguin-like birds which are the largest of our short-winged divers. A compact body and neck, sharp pointed bill, small wings, and short tail. The sexes are colored alike, a rich brownish-black above, and white below. Common throughout the year, but in winter they often travel in large flocks up and down the coast, in spring laying their single, pear-shaped eggs on sea cliffs and rocky islands. The very attentive parents turn their dark brown backs to the sea to protect the eggs and, once the eggs hatch, to protect the chicks from predators. As the chicks reach the flight stage, the parents signal the young to leave their nests. Kerawk! Kerawk! Suddenly, those very little birds on those very high cliffs drop to the water, miraculously with no damage at all.

A group of small, chunky seabirds, the Marbled Murrelets, *Brachyramphus marmoratus*, squats patiently on the rocks just below the cliffs. In summer the dark brown plumage of both sexes is sparsely "marbled" with white below; by winter the plumage changes: blackish above, whitish below, with white stripes above the wings and a white collar at the back of the neck. Resident Marbled Murrelets sometimes gather in hundreds off our coast, but have long been regarded as mysterious seabirds. Even their breeding haunts remained a puzzle solved only recently: unlike most seabirds, they build their mossy nests several miles inland in the tops of large Douglas Fir trees, raise their young at the nesting site until they are capable of flight, and then arrive on the sea toward the end of June. Marbled Murrelets have perfect camouflage: during the spring and summer breeding season their brown-specked bodies blend with the dry interior forest, but when the birds return to the sea the black above and white below provide good camouflage against the sea and sky.

Marbled Murrelet
summer

Whole colonies of pigeon-like birds, the Pigeon Guillemots, *Cepphus columba*, live in the crevices along the cliffs and on offshore islands. Their black bodies, large white wing patches, and bright red feet and mouth are unmistakable, but in winter the black is almost replaced by white. They often sit upright, penguin style, as though embarrassed by their awkwardness on land. But those in the air gracefully ride the upcurrents and, quick as a wink, dive deep below the surface of the water where they steer with their feet and propel themselves with out-stretched wings while feeding on shellfish and small fishes, especially blennies and sculpins.

Pigeon Guillemot

Silhouetted against the rocks on more protected cliffs, and occasionally in some of the tree-tops, the Double-crested Cormorants, *Phalacrocorax auritus*, sit patiently upright. These rather large, long-necked birds are solid black with shiny greenish "iridescent" reflections and yellow faces. Their messy nests situated among the guano covered rocks are of sticks, branches, and roots, and lined with seaweeds and other shoreline debris. Each nest contains three or four pale blue eggs. When newly hatched, the naked young are coal black; brownish juveniles have pale underparts. Double-crested Cormorants are the only ones found inland, where the colonies sit in trees.

Double-crested
Cormorant

A smaller cormorant occurs in even greater numbers on the rocks and islands offshore, the Pelagic Cormorant, *Phalacrocorax pelagicus*. They enter the water headfirst, without the slightest splash, and once under they swim with extraordinary speed and easily capture speedy fish. Their plumage is not well protected against the water, and after about forty seconds they bring their prey to the surface where, with the delicate look of true connoisseurs, they toss the fish into the air and let them slide down their long throats head first. And then, as though to draw attention to themselves, with wings outstretched the birds sit upright on crags or rocks or buoys and wait for the warm sun to dry their water-logged plumage.

Pelagic Cormorant

A mischievous band of all-black birds fills the air with loud nasal "caws": the familiar Northwestern Crow, *Corvus caurinus*, walks briskly among the debris at the high tide line. The Northwestern Crow appears to be an identical sub species of the slightly larger inland Common Crow, but the Northwestern Crow lives only along the coast, in the coniferous trees and in shrubs above the beaches. When the tide drops, they come down to the seashore in droves to clean the beaches of any edible items washed up by the sea, such as dead fish, crabs, and shellfish. They are active predators on sea urchins, whelks and other snails, and small fish such as blennies and sculpins. These crows also spend their time scavenging along with the gulls in garbage dumps and in farmers' fields for grasshoppers, grains, and fruits. They harrass ducks and even gulls to make them regurgitate their catch, and feed heavily on the eggs of other shorebirds, a habit making them unpopular among song-bird lovers and intolerant sportsmen. Crows are one of the most intelligent of birds, wary, adaptive, and well able to survive in all conditions. Opportunistic and known as "black robbers", they are one of the most conspicuous and interesting birds at the seashore.

Northwestern Crow

Tripping daintily among the rocks, and occasionally giving loud, flute-like calls to herald their arrival, a pair of Wandering Tattlers, *Heteroscelus incanus*, busily search among the debris looking for food, continuously bobbing and teetering as they work along. Medium-sized shorebirds with yellow legs, their plumage a salty gray with intense black markings along the throat, breast, and flanks; in the fall, duller, with a loss of the intense black and gray markings. These vagabond birds travel alone or in groups of two or three, and range widely, turning up on the coral beaches of the South Seas one season, and the desolate cliffs of the Aleutian Islands the next. The Wandering Tattler is well named, the "tattling" probably originating from their habit of bobbing and teetering. Never very numerous, but they occur regularly along our rocky coast during the spring migration.

Wandering Tattler

59

Suddenly, in swift precision, a pair of Black Oystercatchers, *Haematopus bachmani*, circle the shore and execute several highly skilled manoeuvers before settling to the rocks to look for food. These not-to-be mistaken clowns of the seashore are easily recognized by their jet black plumage, long pink legs and feet, bright red chisel-shaped bills, and golden eyes. The plumage is alike on both the adult male and female, but young birds are brown and their bills are dull. Black Oystercatchers are famous for their acting abilities: they will feign a broken wing or play games of "peek-a-boo" with gulls and other birds that invade their nests. They pry limpets, chitons, snails, and other shellfish off the rocks with the quick flick of their long bills.

Black Oystercatcher

Another captivating rocky shorebird that skips energetically from rock to rock is the Black Turnstone, *Arenaria melanocephala*, a rather small, plump bird about the size of a robin. Its plumage enables it to stand unnoticed on barnacle-covered rocks: black head, breast, and back; black bill and feet; a white spot before the eye; and white speckling. The Black Turnstone searches among the kelp and debris for tiny shellfish and other creatures to eat, and turns over stones of surprising size by inserting its bill under the edge, giving a quick flip, and rolling them away.

Black Turnstone

Amidst the spume and spray of the surf a group of amazing little birds rides the breakers and flits about from one projecting rock to another. These wonderfully agile Surfbirds, *Aphriza virgata*, are slightly larger than the Turnstones, and have dark gray heads, gray breasts with black V-shaped markings, and white tails bearing a conspicuous black band. Common on the outer coast during the fall, winter, and early spring, in April or May they begin to move northward to Alaska where they breed and build their nests on the rocky talus slopes of alpine forests.

Surfbird

Flying low over the surface of the water, in single file goes a flock of long slender ducks with slim bills and dark crested heads, the Red-breasted Mergansers, *Mergus serrator*. The males are exceptionally beautiful, being black and having a green glossy head and upper neck, prominent scraggly crest, rusty-red breast streaked with black, distinct white collar, and white wing patches. The females are drab gray above and white below, with cinnamon-brown neck, head, and crest, and white wing patches ornamented with a black bar. The eyes, bill, and legs of the males are bright red; those of the females, dull. Mergansers are rapid swimmers and expert divers and regularly fish in the surf offshore, feeding mostly on fish and following spawning herring and salmon by the thousands. The hooked and coarsely toothed bill used for holding slippery fish gives the Red-breasted Merganser the popular names "sawbill" or "fisherman duck". In breeding season they migrate to the far north to build their nests near fresh-water lakes and streams or near protected salt water bays, and are common winter ducks along our coast.

Red-breasted Merganser

A flock of large, heavily built birds with peculiarly swollen bills, ride the waves in the offshore kelp beds, the Surf Scoters, *Melanitta perspicillata*. The males are all black with two sharply defined triangular white patches, one on the back of the head and the other on the forehead. The drake's particularly swollen and grotesque bill gives the appearance of his having received the deciding blow in a domestic argument. The adult females resemble juveniles, but the face patches are more obscure than those of the male and there is a patch on the back of the head. Surf Scoters spend most of their lives at sea where they congregate in large flocks; in the summer only the males and non-breeding females are present, the breeding females being on the inland marshes to attend the young. They are expert divers, submerging considerable depths for small mussels, clams, oysters, and fish which, remarkably, they swallow whole.

male

female

Surf Scoter

Nearby a similar group of heavy black ducks rise and run laboriously along the surface of the water to gain momentum, but once airborne these largest of our ducks are strong and steady, the White-winged Scoters, *Melanitta deglandi*. The males are velvet black and usually, but not always, have a small white tear-shaped patch extending down from the eye. The species is easily distinguished from the Surf Scoter; the White-winged Scoter has white wing patches, except that at a distance it often appears to be completely black because the flank feathers sometimes hide the white patch on the folded wings.

White-winged Scoter

Beyond the breakers rides a distinctly colored group of medium-sized ducks with yellow eyes, the Common Golden-eyes, *Bucephala clangula*, commonly called "Whistlers" because of the vibrant whistling sounds made by their wings while in flight. The males are a striking black and white with a head glossed with a beautiful iridescent green, and a round white spot between the eye and bill; the females are lighter, having brown heads, white necks and undersides, and grayish back and sides; the feet of both are yellow. Golden-eyes feed by plucking barnacles, snails, and crabs off rocks or by diving under water to catch small fishes, and playfully chase each other back and forth in the water as though playing a game of tag. Occasionally the entire group rises off the water, flies rapidly in circles to gain altitude, and then, with penetrating whistle sounds, dives from great heights into the sea.

male

About a dozen birds of similar appearance and behavior frolic in the waves nearby, occasionally stopping to dive to considerable depths to hunt for shellfish which they swallow beneath the water, and then surface after long intervals — Barrow's Golden-eyes, *Bucephala islandica*. The species can be distinguished from the Common Golden-eye because the white patch between the eye and bill of the male Barrow's Golden-eye is crescent-shaped instead of round, the head glossed with purple instead of green, and the bill shorter and more pointed. The flight is similar also, but the sound of the Barrow's is neither so loud nor so metallic. An outstanding difference, too, is that the comparatively tame and trusting Barrow's seem to show little fear of man. Both species winter on the coast, but in early spring begin the voyage inland to their breeding grounds in the Rocky Mountains.

female

Common Golden-eye

Barrow's Golden-eye

Flashing beyond the breakers — the distinctly hooded heads of a perky troup of Horned Grebes, *Podiceps auritus*. During the summer both the male and female have a rich chestnut neck and flanks and black head with a striking golden-yellow bar running through the eye and extending over the hood; in winter the hind neck and mantle are dull gray, almost black, and the underside silvery white. Grebes are strictly water birds, having paddle-like feet placed far to the back; flattened, almost tailless bodies; and thick layers of down. They glide over the water without making a ripple and then dive effortlessly, with their wings tightly folded, to feed upon small marine animals, particularly shrimp and small fish.

Horned Grebe

Gently nearby bob graceful swan-like ducks with long sinuous necks and long slender, pointed bills, Western Grebes, *Aechmophorus occidentalis*, commonly called "Swan Grebes". Both sexes are a contrasting black above and white below with a black cap descending in a sharp line down the neck. Like all grebes they spend their lives in the water: expert divers and underwater swimmers they are clumsy and helpless when stranded on land, and may even die unless helped back into the water. Like the Horned Grebes, they winter in large flocks along the coast, but with the coming of spring return to inland lakes and ponds to nest.

Western Grebe

Where the surging surf breaks over stoney shores and offshore rocks, watch for an isolated group of surf-lovers, the brightly colored Harlequin Ducks, *Histrionicus histrionicus*. The males are particularly striking, having chestnut flanks, grayish-blue heads, and sharply contrasting white markings; the females much less attractive, being brown with three small white patches on the head. The females are commonly mistaken for female Surf Scoters, but are smaller and have less conspicuous bills. The males greatly outnumber the females because the mated females stay at home to raise the young near swift moving mountain streams, while the males, accompanied by a few unmated females, spend their summers enjoying the seacoast, but by August or September the young are capable of flight, and the juveniles and mated females return to the sea. The beauty and behavior of these stately wanderers have earned them the common name of "Lord and Lady".

Harlequin Duck (male)

In late fall, one of the last groups of birds to migrate are the happy-go-lucky Oldsquaws, *Clangula hyemalis*, which come in from the north, moving in swift irregular flocks that twist and turn and fly unexpectedly in broad circles. In the distance they are a noisy group, for they continually chatter and gabble about, often with rhythmic musical notes, a trait which has earned them such common names as "old wife", "old squaw", "noisy winter duck", and "organ duck". The small, chunky Oldsquaws are easy to recognize because of their garrulous chatter, their short pinkish bills, and the unmistakably long central tail feathers of the males. In winter the males are mainly white with piebald white and brown markings; the females have a brown mantle, white breast, and piebald head. When searching for food they string out in a long line and at a given signal dive, one at a time, and spend up to two minutes under water probing among the stones for crustaceans, shellfish, and fishes. In early spring the restless merry band starts its northward voyage, chattering and singing all the way.

Harlequin Duck (female)

Oldsquaw

The Spray Zone

Zone 1 The Spray Zone

The Spray Zone is above the High Tide Zone. It is almost completely dry, the upper part being only occasionally sprayed, and the lower part covered with water only during the highest tides and storms.

Plants and animals living on the rocks and in crevices must be able to hold water for long dry periods, and must survive the extreme temperature changes that occur during the heat of the summer and the freezing cold of winter. In addition they must survive rapid changes in salinity, the amount of salt contained in the water. Compared to the lower zones, there are fewer obvious species of plants and animals in the Spray Zone, but those are present in larger numbers.

Just below the area clearly belonging to the land is an area of bare rocks, a no man's land, an area neither truly land nor truly sea. Only a few specialized organisms live here: mites, beetles, spiders and ants scurry about, some having moved down from the land, and some living here all the time; flies, mosquitoes, and tiny wasps hover above the rocks.

In holes on the tops of rocks and in some of the larger crevices there are small pools of water, mostly rainwater because pools this high on the beach only occasionally receive the ocean spray. During the spring and summer many of the fresh-water pools become breeding places for countless beetles, flies, and mosquitoes.

The Spray Zone can be recognized by a band of black lichens covering the rocks, especially in the upper part of the zone. A bright green seaweed, commonly called Sea Hair, almost certainly appears where fresh water seeps down; hordes of little black snails, periwinkles, cover the rocks below the lichens; and species of limpets that survive under hard conditions live in the cracks and crevices. The zone ends before the barnacles begin to appear in their greatest numbers, well above the area where the rockweeds become lush.

On some rock faces high in the zone there is only a wide band of black stain, a zone of encrusting Black Lichens, *Verrucaria maura*. Lichens are made up of two organisms, algae and fungi, which live together in a close partnership, and are so hardy that they are often called "pioneer plants" because they inhabit areas in which no other plants can survive.

Occasionally a Rock Louse, *Ligia pallasii*, may run across the rocks or squeeze tightly into cracks. This large isopod lives very high on the beach, so far from wave action that it seems to be afraid of getting its feet wet. It feeds on detritus, which is the remains of dead plants and animals, and reaches a length of about 3 cm. Look for the Rock Louse at night because it is then that it feeds.

Where fresh water seeps down there will likely be a slender green alga, sometimes known as Sea Hair, and sometimes as Confetti, *Enteromorpha* sp. Often in wide green, yellow, and white patches, it is the same hair-like seaweed that hangs down from the higher rocks and caves, a tubular alga needing considerable moisture to survive. The vivid yellow-green strands survive well in high temperatures during long periods when exposed to the sun, but when the alga dies, it turns white.

Black Lichen

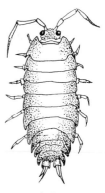

Rock Louse

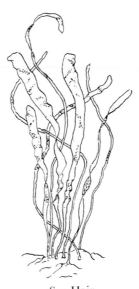

Sea Hair

Photo 90 p. 47

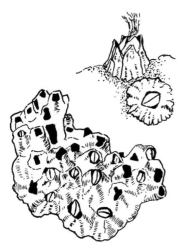

On bare exposed rocks, and crowding into the cracks and crevices, are thousands of little barnacles. They may show no movement or sign of life at all, but when the tide returns and submerges their stony cone-shaped shells, the barnacles thrust a group of feathery plumes in and out. The plume is made up of six appendages, or cirri, and works like a net to sweep the water for microscopic food. Barnacle shells consist of a number of plates: some form the volcano-like wall, and the rest, when drawn together, tightly cover the opening to create a protective moist chamber for the soft animal inside. Barnacles regularly molt, or shed their thin inner covering, to allow room for their bodies to grow, and during the spring and summer their clear cast-off skins float in the quiet waters of protected bays.

Common Acorn Barnacle

Two barnacles are common high up on the rocks. The larger and more abundant is the Common Acorn Barnacle, *Balanus glandula*, which reaches a width of nearly 1.5 cm and has dingy white heavily ribbed plates. Its name is a good one: from the top the central structure looks like an acorn. The other is the very dainty Small Acorn Barnacle, *Chthamalus dalli*, its shell reaching a width of .5 cm and with somewhat darker plates than the Common Acorn Barnacle. The Small Acorn Barnacle has a smooth, rather trim shell, and forms a cross-shaped figure when the four cover plates are pulled tightly together.

Small Acorn Barnacle

Look in cracks and crevices and tidepools just below the black band of lichens where whole herds of small dingy snails crowd together. These periwinkles stay as far away from the sea as possible only occasionally coming barely close enough to wet their gills. Like all snails, they have an operculum, a hard bony plate at the tip of the foot; it closes like a trap door to create a moist home for the snail sealed inside its shell.

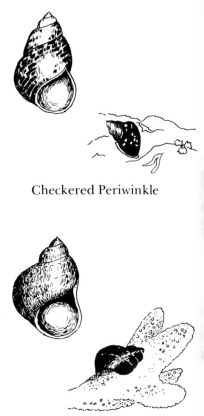

Checkered Periwinkle

Two species of periwinkles occur in the Spray Zone. One is commonly called the Checkered Periwinkle, *Littorina scutulata*, its shell fairly slender and showing a checkerboard pattern of white, brown, and bluish-black, the uppermost whorls a continuous whitish-gray. The largest specimens reach a length of 1 cm. The second species, the Sitka Periwinkle, *Littorina sitkana*, has a shell generally fatter and more squat than that of the Checkered Periwinkle and reaching a length of 1.5 cm. Overall, usually a dull gray, brown, or black, though some specimens show a lighter band of color, variously white, yellow, or orange, on the uppermost whorls.

Sitka Periwinkle

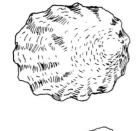

Finger Limpet

Speckled Limpet

Also crowding into the crevices, holes, and tidepools are groups of limpets that look like miniature Chinese hats. Like their relatives the snails, limpets have a muscular foot which they extend when travelling. If the tide is out they plaster themselves against rock with a suction so tight that once they have taken hold prying them off may take a force of up to 32 to 36 kg (70 or 80 pounds). This ability to hold fast to rocks protects the limpets from wave shock and predators and insures a moist chamber inside the shell.

Though there are several species of limpets on rocky shores, the kind usually found with periwinkles is the Finger Limpet, *Collisella digitalis*, its average length about 5 to 12 mm. It can be recognized by its strong ribs and wavy outline, usually brown color and finger-like patches of white streaming down from the top.

Just below the Finger Limpets, around the lower edges of big boulders, watch for the large and rather handsome Speckled Limpet, *Notoacmea persona*, which reaches a length of about 3 to 4 cm and has a somewhat inflated look. Many fine white dots usually speckle its top surface; larger white dots form a butterfly pattern on a band of brown at the base of the shell. The Speckled Limpet feeds on the thin film of algae covering the rocks.

Zone II The High Tide Zone

Immediately below the Spray Zone, the High Tide Zone is subject to much more wave action than the Spray Zone. The upper part of the High Tide Zone, or "Barnacle Zone", has greater numbers and larger sizes of barnacles: incoming waves bring in larvae which settle, cement themselves to the rocks, and grow into adults that can hang onto the rock surfaces even in fast moving water.

There is a greater variety of plants and animals here than in the Spray Zone, although many of the organisms common to the Spray Zone are also present. The Common Acorn Barnacle is abundant, but not the Small Acorn Barnacle; the small clumps of Blue Mussels scattered among the barnacles reach their greatest size and numbers lower down on the beach; limpets and snails are everywhere, and certainly larger and more numerous than in the Spray Zone.

Plants such as Sea Hair appear in the upper part of the zone, mostly where fresh water seeps down from the land. In the middle of the zone the rockweed begins: farther down it grows lushly, and then ends near the Middle Zone. Clumps of bright green Sea Lettuce begin to mingle with the rockweed and on some beaches the beds just below the rockweed are so great that they create a green band. In fact, the whole of the High Tide Zone often looks green from a distance because of the color of so many of the seaweeds.

Shield Limpet

Scattered on the rocks and among the honey-comb of barnacles numerous limpets cling tightly to rocks or creep slowly along in search of food. Their feeding-organ, a "radula", is a long flat ribbon set with horny teeth — a perfect tool for scraping off seaweeds and the thin film of algae covering the rocks.

One of the larger limpets that first appears in the High Tide Zone is the brown and white Shield Limpet, *Collisella pelta*. It is an extremely variable species: sometimes only slightly raised ribs and very wavy bands circle the edge of the shell, but more often it shows a roughly ribbed edge. Large specimens reach a length of 3 or 4 cm.

A similar limpet, the Plate Limpet, *Notoacmea scutum*, has a flatter shell which is never strongly ribbed. Its mottled greenish-gray shell is generally camouflaged with growths of green and brown algae, and has very fine lines running down from the top. It grows to a length of 4 or 5 cm.

Plate Limpet

Towards the lower regions of the zone a new barnacle makes its first appearance, the Thatched Acorn Barnacle, *Balanus cariosus*, its sides having overlapping ridges that look somewhat like a thatched roof. Though it sometimes occurs alone, it may also be clustered. This interesting species varies greatly in shape and appearance, depending on the conditions in its habitat: in solitary specimens the shell is usually a steep-walled thatched cone with numerous downward ridges, but crowded specimens have longer cones with less of a thatched appearance. The size also varies greatly, from 2 to 4 cm across and 3 to 6 cm high. Young or uncrowded specimens are white; older crowded specimens a dirty gray.

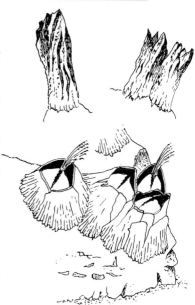

Thatched Acorn Barnacle

On the open coast the cracks and crevices often contain great clusters of Black Turban Snails, *Tegula funebralis*, an appropriate name for a shell shaped much like an East Indian headdress or turban. When wet the shells are shiny black, but when dry the shells are dingy black, blending in very well with the surrounding rocks. The top is usually worn and variously colored; it may have a pearly white, brown, or black surface tinged with green, purple, or pink, or it may be covered with an encrusting pink algae. On shores exposed to a fair amount of wave action, the Black Turban is the most common snail in the High Tide Zone.

Black Turban Snail

Towards the middle of the High Tide Zone the Rockweeds, *Fucus* sp., begin to grow in bushy clumps, lying flat across the rocks or hanging down in curtains, and keeping the wetness in and under them. Olive-green, often with yellowish tips, and reaching a length of 30 cm, rockweeds often have conspicuous floating air bladders in the surface layers in which they grow their eggs. Several different species occur, the size and shape of each plant greatly affected by its habitat.

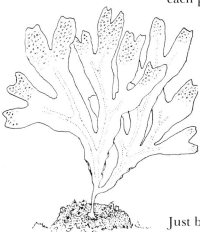

Rockweed

Photo 84 p. 46

Just below the rockweeds a bright emerald-green seaweed called Sea Lettuce, or *Ulva*, looks like leaf lettuce with thin wide wrinkled fronds. In the High Tide Zone, Sea Lettuce usually grows in tidepools, but large patches are more common low in this zone and high in the Middle Zone. When the tide drops the sun dries the seaweed and it looks and feels like crisp tissue paper. Eat raw Sea Lettuce after washing it in fresh water to remove the strong salty taste.

Sea Lettuce

Photo 88 p. 46

Another very common seaweed high on the shore and extremely abundant where the surf beats, Sea Moss, *Endocladia muricata*, looks like tufts of dark brownish-red or blackish-brown moss, the tufts being bushy and small, generally not more than 3 cm high.

Sea Moss
Photo 85 p. 46

A peculiar blackish or brownish seaweed hangs rather sparingly from the upper surfaces of boulders: Bald Sea Hair, *Bangia fuscopurpurea*. When the tide falls, the 2 to 10 cm-long silken strands spread out over the rocks in such a way that the seaweed looks like the thinning hairs of a bald-headed man. Sometimes, though, this seaweed does occur in dense patches.

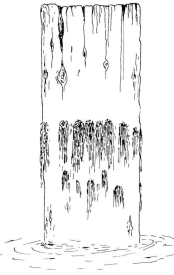

Bald Sea Hair

A group of snails range from the High Tide Zone to the Low Tide Zone, the whelks. Unlike the limpets and periwinkles which feed on algae, whelks are carnivores which feed on barnacles and mussels. Whelks drill neat circular holes in the shells of their prey by using a special rasping device, the radula, and with a shell-dissolving secretion from the underside of the foot. The snail alternately drills and dissolves the shell until the hole is complete. The whelk extends its proboscis through the hole and the radula tears out the soft body of the prey and the food is carried into the body of the snail for digestion.

Rock Whelk

A very colorful whelk growing to 2.5 cm and living in the open as well as in crevices, and in beds of seaweeds, is the Rock Whelk, *Thais emarginata*. Its shell is made up of three whorls with strongly developed raised ribs which are usually white, the lines between them variously colored yellow, orange, brown, gray, or black. A similar species but one larger, a little more slender, and less brightly colored, the Channeled Whelk, *Thais canaliculata*, has very distinct ribs which are closer together and all colored alike, generally a dull whitish gray. It reaches a length of about 3 or 4 cm.

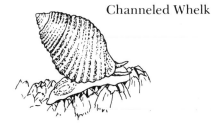

Channeled Whelk

During the spring and summer large numbers of animals, such as small snails, limpets, isopods, amphipods, and crabs, live beneath the rockweeds or in the beds of eelgrass where the fronds and stems provide protection from shore predators and from the drying sun. In addition, the presence of a wide variety of organisms provides food for each species.

An interesting group of hardy animals often found in the rockweeds, or where decaying seaweeds accumulate, isopods have long, flattened bodies, usually with seven pairs of short legs of about equal size. Most isopods are quite small, less than 4 cm in length, and feed on diatoms, detritus, seaweeds, and the eggs of seashore animals.

Rockweed Isopod

Two species are common to the High Tide Zone. One is the rather handsome Rockweed Isopod, *Idotea wosnesenskii*, up to 4 cm long. It is well camouflaged against the rockweeds, being generally of the same olive-green color. Rockweed Isopods are remarkable "acrobatic" swimmers: watch them at night with a flashlight for then they come out of the seaweeds to scavenge for food in the tidepools.

A very small chubby isopod about 1 cm long, the drab gray Oregon Pill Bug lives among the seaweeds, especially where there is considerable seepage of fresh water. What the Pill Bug lacks in size it makes up by a long Latin name, *Gnorimosphaeroma oregonensis*, and its large numbers — many hundreds to the square meter. Hold one in your hand; watch the isopod roll up into a tight round ball.

Oregon Pill Bug

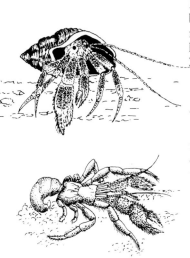

Here and there are calm pools of water with sea-weeds lining their walls and casting deep shadows. Limpets, barnacles, and periwinkles live on the bottom. Among the barnacles cluster small specimens of mussels; these same mussels become larger and more abundant in the Middle Tide Zone.

The hermit crabs will probably attract attention first, amusing creatures which never lose interest in their lifelong search for a suitable home. Because their lower abdomen is soft and curled, as they grow they must constantly find larger shells to protect their bodies. The hermits, therefore, often fight vicious-looking battles over empty snail shells. If time permits, a hermit will grasp the new shell, turn it around, tap it with the antennae, and look inside. The inspection completed, the hermit quickly hops out of the old shell and slides tail first into the new one, and uses hook-like appendages for holding onto the "shellhouse" and the large claws for blocking the entrance to the shell.

Hairy Hermit Crab

Photo 2 p. 18

Several species of hermit crabs occur intertidally, but two occur most frequently in the High Tide Zone. One of the more common species is the Hairy Hermit Crab, *Pagurus hirsutiusculus*, recognized by its hairiness and by the white or blue band around the base of the legs of larger specimens. Along with the Hairy Hermit Crab, but becoming more abundant lower down on the shore, the Granular Hermit Crab, *Pagurus granosimanus*, is about the same size as the Hairy Hermit but is almost hairless. Its pinchers are rough and granular, its legs spotted with white or blue bands, its antennae red.

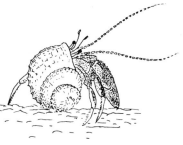

Granular Hermit Crab

In the bottom of the pool several very small strange-looking fish will glide from rock to rock — Tidepool Sculpins, *Oligocottus maculosus*, their heads very large for their small tapering bodies, their large forward fins apparently used for walking. Well camouflaged Tidepool Sculpins blend beautifully with the rocks, weeds, and shadows of the pool. Colors vary greatly, but they usually include some shades of black, brown, or green along with some white. Younger ones show more white than do the adults which may reach a length of about 10 cm.

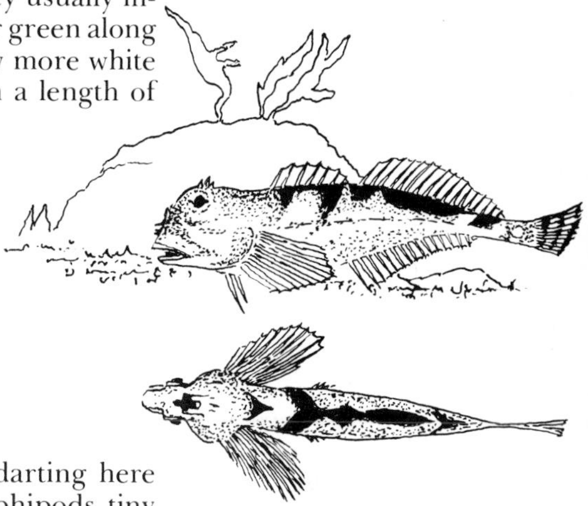

Tidepool Sculpin

Photo 80 p. 44

Clinging to the bottom and busily darting here and there are herds of Kelp Fleas, amphipods, tiny animals about 5 mm to 1.5 cm in length, generally a dull green or gray-brown with short antennae. Sometimes called "sideswimmers", they swim on their flattened sides and scavenge on detritus, the dead matter on the bottom. Many species of amphipods, each equipped for a different habitat, live in tidepools, among seaweeds, and in the open sea, and because of their small size and enormous numbers they are the food of countless larger animals.

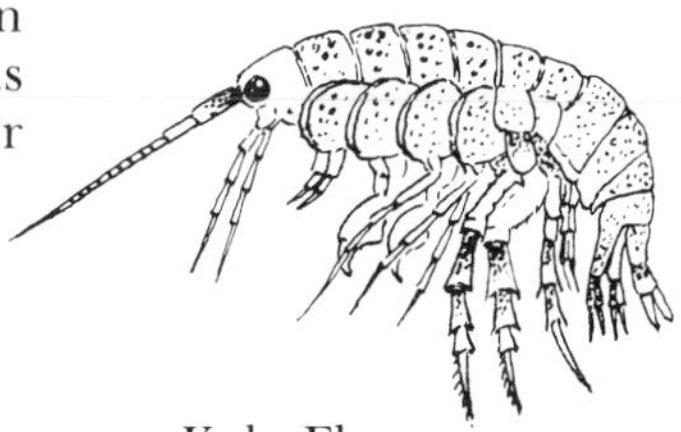

Kelp Flea

Photo 12 p. 20

Tiny Tube Worm

Flatworm

Turn over rocks just above and just below the rockweeds. Some of the rocks may be small and round, and always wet because they are in little pools of water, the underside likely covered with the hard white tubes of the strange-looking Tiny Tube Worm, *Spirorbis* spp. The tube consists of calcium carbonate, chemically the same as limestone, marble, and the hard white material in teeth. The tentacles extending from the tube of an undisturbed worm are bright red, and disappear instantly whenever the rock to which the worm is cemented is moved. The tubes are generally coiled and are only 2 or 3 mm in diameter and 2 or 3 cm in length.

Another very peculiar group of animals is common on the undersides of rocks, the Flatworm Turbellarians, of which there are many different species. Generally tape-flat, oval, or circular, their bodies are about twice as long as wide. The color varies, but the common brownish-gray blends well with the under-rock habitat. Flatworms are particularly noticeable during the spring and summer when both the worms and their jelly-like egg cases cling to the undersides of moist rocks. They can move and swim with surprising speed by ruffling the margins of the body.

On most rocky shores watch the hundreds of shore crabs scramble to hide under the rocks. Shore crabs propel themselves sideways as they search the rocks for food. Together with other scavengers of the intertidal zones they recycle waste matter, and act as garbage disposal systems by removing unwanted waste materials from the seashore.

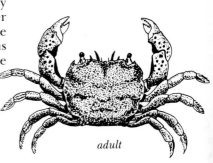

adult

On well drained beaches where boulders rest on sand or gravel the Purple Shore Crab, *Hemigrapsus nudus*, will likely be present, its nearly rectangular body measuring 4 or 5 cm across. Usually reddish or reddish-purple, the adult can be distinguished from the Oregon Rock Crab because the Purple Shore Crab has a number of distinct purple spots on the pinchers. Small specimens come in great varieties of color, and have intriguing white designs on their carapaces.

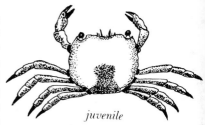

juvenile

Purple Shore Crab
Photo 3 p. 18

Hiding under pebbles and bits of gravel the wide-ranging Green Shore Crab, *Hemigrapsus oregonensis*, is abundant on rocky, cobbley, and muddy beaches, mostly where fresh water comes into the shore. Generally 3 or 4 cm across the carapace, it is a smaller edition of the similarly shaped Purple Shore Crab of the rocky shore, but adult Green Shore Crabs have hairy fringed legs. They are duller in color — yellowish to olive-gray — and their claws lack the purple dots.

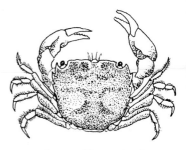

Green Shore Crab

81

High Cockscomb

Under rocks the size of cobblestones is a group of writhing eel-like fish called blennies, their long top dorsal fin running into the tail and making the blennies look like eels. One of the more plentiful species is the High Cockscomb, *Anoplarchus purpurescens.* This blenny is really not so homely as it might appear at first: a combination of browns, grays, blacks, and greens, and designs or stripes run the length of the body. The largest may reach a length of 30 cm.

Here, also, are the little Northern Clingfish, *Gobiesox maeandricus*, which slither over damp surfaces and stubbornly cling to the undersides of rocks with special fins that form a powerful suction device. The large flat head seems to taper to the tail, and the body changes color to blend in with the surroundings. The size varies from 8 to 15 cm. As long as blennies and clingfish have the protection of their under-rock habitat, they can survive until the incoming tide. Place them back under the rocks.

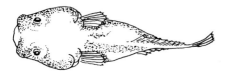

Northern Clingfish

Zone III The Middle Tide Zone

The Middle Tide Zone lies immediately below the High Tide Zone, and contains more animals and plants than the higher zones. Tidal action uncovers this area twice each day, and the changes in temperature and salinity are less pronounced because of the longer periods under water. Lush plant growth provides protection from the deadly sunlight for animals requiring a moist habitat. Rockweeds will still be present, but not likely so many as in the High Tide Zone. Sea Lettuce is also still here and sometimes in great patches. And a new group of fleshy seaweeds, the Sea Cabbage, Sea Cauliflower, and Sea Sac, hold in moisture during periods of low tide.

On protected shores the beginning of the zone is marked by Edible Blue Mussels, but on the outer coast the California Blue Mussel and the Goose Neck Barnacle attach to rocks. On both shores the Common Purple or Ochre Sea Star preys heavily on mussel beds everywhere. In addition several species of snails, limpets, and chitons cling to the rocks, crevices, and overhangs. Some species always live in the lower zones, others live offshore in deeper water and move up onto the shore.

Edible Blue Mussel

High in this zone, either clumped together or sharing spaces with the barnacles lie great beds of mussels, bivalves with two shells hinged together by an elastic ligament. They attach themselves to rocks and to each other with long elastic threads called "byssus threads" which allow the mussels to cluster together in holes and in crevices until masses hang down over the rocks. Mussels move very slowly, the byssus and the foot working together. Like the barnacles, mussels are filter feeders and during high tides open their shells and filter the water for microscopic food.

On shores protected from strong wave action there will almost certainly be clumps of Edible Blue Mussels, *Mytilus edulis*, often called the "Bay Mussel" because it prefers quiet waters. It survives well in estuaries near fresh-water streams where the salinity is considerably lower than that of full-strength sea water. A fairly small mussel with a smooth wedge-shaped shell rarely longer than 6 cm in length.

On many surf-swept beaches on the outer coast, the California Blue Mussel, *Mytilus californianus*, reaches a length of 20 to 25 cm. The handsome heavily ribbed shell is blue, brown, and black; internally the shell is slightly iridescent and generally blue-gray in color. The bright orange flesh is edible. A few specimens contain tiny pearls, but they are of no value.

California Blue Mussel

With the beds of California Blue Mussels there will almost certainly be thick colonies of the Goose Neck Barnacle, *Pollicipes polymerus*. The leathery stalk, or "neck", generally about 2 cm, and the upper part of the body covered with plates of varying sizes; the stalk brown to red; the plates white. The Goose Neck Barnacle is adapted for life in a violent world: its tough elastic stalk bends back and forth with the surf. Stay well away from the breaking waves when examining these species because the California Blue Mussel and the Goose Neck Barnacle live where unpredictably strong currents and rushing waves beat the shore.

On the rocks just below the mussel beds, and occasionally stranded in the higher zones, are many kinds of brightly colored sea stars. By far the most abundant is the Common Purple or Ochre Star, *Pisaster ochraceus*, large specimens growing to about 40 cm across. This sea star is harsh to the touch because its body has many blunt limy spines. The color varies greatly, possibly because of the environmental differences between a sheltered shoreline and one exposed to considerable wave action: specimens on the surf-swept outer coast are generally orange, those in more protected and more northerly waters generally purple.

Noted for its appetite, that Common Purple or Ochre Star humped up over a clam, mussel, or oyster is probably positioning itself over the shellfish to eat it. When attacking a shellfish, the sea star uses its tube feet to pull and pull until slowly the two muscles holding the shells together begin to tire and start to gape slightly. The sea star quickly slips its stomach from itself into the shellfish; the stomach secretes digestive enzymes, and as the tissues of the prey soften, the sea star extends its bag-shaped stomach farther into the open spaces and digests the animal right inside its own shell. This digestive process may take two or three days.

Goose Neck Barnacle

Common Purple
or Ochre Star
Photo 53 p. 32

Several species of plants and animals live in the spaces between the mussels and barnacles to protect themselves from the drying sun and the force of the waves. The incoming tides provide plankton for the filter-feeding barnacles, for mussels, and for the tube worms and small clams. A thin film of algae and detritus covers everything and provides food for grazing animals such as snails and limpets. Dig down and separate some of the mussels; in the spaces find the snails, limpets, isopods, amphipods, worms, and small crabs.

Intertwined among the barnacles and mussels are several species of gaily colored nemerteans, or "ribbon worms", thin elastic worms that stretch to several times their normal length. Most nemerteans break apart at the slightest disturbance, but each piece, if larger than a centimeter, may develop into a complete new animal. Although nemerteans appear to be very soft and sluggish they can capture a variety of larger, more vicious-looking, almost armored, worms. The nemertean can extend its proboscis, or tube-like "mouth", to great distances, and some species have a proboscis armed with a paralyzing poison which enables the nemertean to swallow the victim whole.

One nemertean occurs in great coiled masses, the Green Nemertean, *Emplectonema gracile*, a long slender worm looking something like a green rubber band. When fully extended it reaches 15 to 20 cm, but when contracted it may be only 2 or 3 cm. Dark above, and white or yellow below. Not so likely as some species to break apart when handled.

A strikingly obvious, but uncommon nemertean in mussel beds, the Orange Nemertean, *Tubulanus polymorphus*, is bright reddish-orange, parts of it sometimes as thick as a pencil, and a meter or more in length when fully stretched out.

Green Nemertean

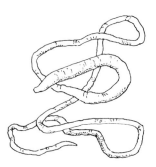

Orange Nemertean

On the tops and sides of boulders, and in crevices and holes, small green sea anemones may cover the rocks so thickly that Aggregate Anemone, *Anthopleura elegantissima*, is an appropriate name. When fully expanded large specimens are about 4 cm across and not much more than 2.5 cm in height. Greenish with pink-to-purple-tipped tentacles. Though common in the middle and lower zones this species sometimes lives in the High Tide Zone, especially where the falling tide has left stranded pools of water. Aggregate Anemones are so hardy that they can live on rocks exposed to sun, waves, and wind. They open fully when covered with water and exposed to sunlight and cover themselves with bits of gravel and shell, and when contracted they blend with the background.

Aggregate Anemone
Photo 71 p. 40

A variety of chitons cling tightly to the rocks and crevices, and adhere to the bottom of tidepools in the middle and lower zones, but the only chiton nearly always present in the Middle Tide Zone is the Black Chiton, *Katharina tunicata*, the second largest on our Northwest coast, growing to about 10 cm in length. Unlike other chitons lower down, this one is often in plain sight, exposed for long periods to the drying sun. Like the snails and limpets, chitons have a large flat muscular foot by which they cling stubbornly to rocks, and which, together with the body which is a leathery girdle, allows the chiton to adhere tightly to irregular surfaces. Use a pocket knife to dislodge one, pick it up, and watch it roll into a round ball to protect itself. That large, dull, yellowish muscle on the underside is the foot.

Black Chiton
Photo 28 p. 25

Sea Cauliflower

The globular mass of a peculiar light brown or yellowish seaweed of this middle zone, the Sea Cauliflower or Brain Seaweed, *Leathesia difformis*, somewhat resembles a miniature brain or a small stalk of cauliflower. This one appears in the spring and disintegrates in the fall. When the tide drops the thick globular mass of filaments keeps the wetness in.

Another one that is odd and abundant in this zone is Sea Cabbage, *Hedophyllum sessile*. In sheltered waters it looks something like an old head of cabbage, but actually it is one large thick corrugated and tattered blade wrapped around itself. On the open coast it is very different: the blades are generally smooth, narrow, and deeply split, a form thought to offer less resistance to wave action and less likely to be torn apart. Both reach a length of 50 cm.

Sea Cabbage

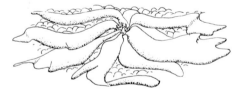

The surprising Sea Sac, *Halosaccion glandiforme*, is a cluster of hollow, olive-brown or yellowish-brown, thin-walled little sacs filled completely or nearly completely with water. A gas-filled part at the top of the sac makes the seaweed buoyant and enables it to stand erect. The sacs are from 10 to 20 cm long and 2 to 3 cm wide. Gently squeeze the seaweed to squirt fine sprays of water through little holes at the top.

A very graceful olive-brown seaweed resembling a small palm tree, the Sea Palm, *Postelsia palmaeformis*, lives fairly high on the shore, but only on the open coast where surf is strong. The upright hollow stem measures up to 60 cm: near the top as many as 100 strap-shaped blades, 1 to 3 cm wide and 25 cm long; a holdfast of numerous short root-like structures. The strong holdfast attaches firmly to rocks, and the hollow but flexible stem allows for swaying back and forth with the beating waves in a really wild surf-swept world.

This distinctive seaweed indicates that the area is dangerous!

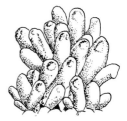

Sea Sac
Photo 89 p. 46

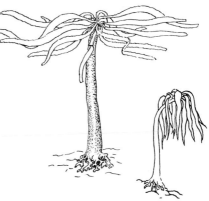

Sea Palm
Photo 92 p. 47

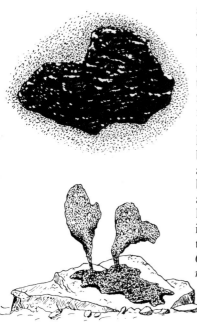

On some of the rocks in the High Tide and Middle Tide Zone strange black blotches looking like tar spots appear to be leakage from passing oil tankers. Fortunately these blotches may only be Sea Tar, an odd algae, *Petrocelis middendorffii*, the blotches black or purplish-gray when dry, but tending to be slightly reddish when covered by the tide. Generally wide-spread they measure 1 or 2 mm high and 6 cm across, though some cover a meter or more. Find it throughout the year, but most commonly in the spring and summer. The life cycle of this seaweed has long been a mystery, but biologists now believe that the black blotches are actually a phase in the life cycle of a dark brownish-red to almost black seaweed on rocks and in tidepools in the lower zones, formerly known as *Gigartina papillata*, but more recently identified as *Petrocelis middendorffii*. It seems likely that other plants now considered to be species of *Gigartina* may really be phases in the life of *Petrocelis*, or some other seaweed.

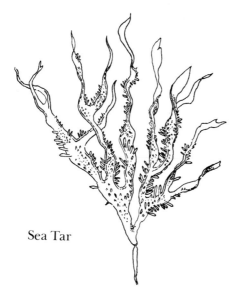

Sea Tar

A reddish-brown seaweed fairly high on the beach, often as high as the rockweeds, is Crisp Leather, *Gigartina cristata*, up to 8 cm in height. The flattened, often twisted, leathery blades occur in bushy clusters in both the High Tide Zone and the Middle Tide Zone. Small outgrowths covering the surface of the blades make the seaweed look like a rough coarse towel. When the tide drops and the seaweed dries, the blades often become crisp and turn blackish.

Crisp Leather

A similar seaweed among the rockweeds prefers the open coast, the Rough Strap, *Gigartina harveyana*. This intriguing species has a long narrow blade tending to be rectangular, and with numerous elongated branchlets along the edge. The surface of the main blade is profusely covered with rough, often twisted, outgrowths, and the blade looks and feels like coarse sandpaper. Reddish-brown or reddish-purple, the length up to 15 cm, the width 3 or 4 cm.

A larger species, Turkish Towel, more blade-like and unbranched, occurs lower on the shore.

Rough Strap

Black Pine

A seaweed that looks and feels to the touch very much like an old twisted rope is commonly called Black Pine, *Rhodomela larix*, about 20 cm in length. Its name comes from the tufts of short, spiralling branchlets which give the appearance of pine needles. When dry this seaweed is jet black, but in water it is a dirty brown dish-water color. The appearance of Black Pine changes dramatically with the seasons: in winter the short spiralling branchlets drop off, and leave the long main stem standing stiff and naked.

A bushy reddish-brown to almost black type occurs with Black Pine, Sea Brush, *Odonthalia floccosa*, and grows to 30 or 40 cm. The four species on our coast are difficult to tell apart, but Sea Brush can be identified by the small holdfast. The major stems are profusely branched, and have alternately arranged small stubby branchlets that frequently appear tightly knotted near the tips. The stubby branchlets give the seaweed a flat bushy appearance. Examine the stiff bushy stems of Black Pine and Sea Brush because both provide shelter for a variety of very tiny animals, especially for amphipods.

Sea Brush

Coralline algae grows on rocks exposed to the open coast and particularly on rocks lining tidepools — strange-looking, coral-like plants usually reddish-pink or purplish-pink, sometimes with whitish fringes. Difficult to think of them as seaweeds? They are, but made of calcium, the same material as in seashells, teeth, and bones. Generally, coralline algae are brittle and hard or rock-like to the touch. The segments are calcified, but the joints between them are not and allow for a flexibility that enables the algae to sway with the current. Though some species live in the Middle Tide Zone, the family as a whole is more common in the Low Tide Zone and in deeper offshore water.

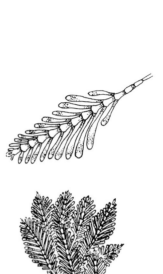

One of the more common species is pale pink to bright pink with flattened lace-like branches, Graceful Coral Seaweed, *Corallina vancouveriensis*. The densely crowded branches are longer than they are wide, the upright part up to 5 or 7 cm high. When fertile the tips of the branches swell and give the seaweed a graceful feather-like appearance; when exposed to strong sunlight, or when dying, it bleaches to white or light pink. Branches frequently float with the debris at the High Tide Zone.

Graceful Coral Seaweed
Photo 86 p. 46

A very unusual group of reddish-pink coralline algae are the Coral Leaf Seaweeds, *Bossiella* sp., 4 to 10 cm tall. Four similar species of *Bossiella* occur on our coast, but they all have an irregular system of jointed segments, thick broadly rounded and flattened leaf-like branches, and they are all brittle. When fertile the reproductive structures are in little bumps on the surface of the segments.

Coral Leaf Seaweed
Photo 87 p. 46

A coralline alga that encrusts the rocks and looks like peculiar splotches of reddish-pink or purplish paint, Rock Crust, *Lithothamnium philippi*, is roughly circular in shape and 4 to 10 cm across. It grows 1 to 4 mm high and may have raised ridges or may be smooth or may be covered with small knobs. The rough hard Rock Crust also covers the shells of snails, limpets, and other hard-shelled animals in the middle and lower zones.

Rock Crust
Photo 20 p. 21

Hanging down from the rocks and in particular lining permanently submerged tidepools on the outer coast, great tangled masses of Surfgrass, *Phyllospadix scouleri*, generally grow as long as a meter. From a distance the long, narrow blades, 3 cm wide, look like rich green grass and resemble the eelgrass of the higher zones. Surfgrass is not an alga; it is related to true grasses.

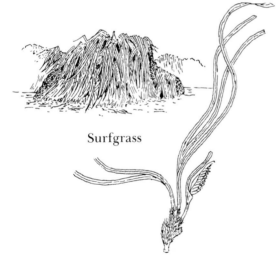

Surfgrass

A number of snails and snail relatives cling to the rocks, and live in crevices and on the overhangs of the middle and lower tide zones. One of the most beautiful on both protected and exposed shores is the Wrinkled Whelk, *Thais lamellosa*, some having light fragile and very ornamental shells, others extremely heavy and showing few frills and ornaments. The shell, usually seven whorls and reaching a length of 4 to 7 cm, may be white, yellow, orange, purple, brown, or gray. In the spring and summer look for the large clusters of their yellow egg cases on the undersides of moist rocks. Commonly called "sea oats", the egg cases are the size of large oat grains.

Another fairly long whelk on rocks and in calm pools, the Spindle Whelk, *Searlesia dira*, has a spindle-shaped shell with five or six rounded whorls and rather fine, spiral, raised ridges. Dull in color, generally deep gray or brownish-gray, it reaches a length of 3 or 4 cm. The Spindle Whelk is both a carnivore and a scavenger.

Wrinkled Whelk
Photo 14 p. 21 & Photo 21 p. 22

Spindle Whelk
Photo 13 p. 21

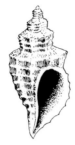

A snail with an interesting spindle-shaped shell, the Sculptured Rock Whelk, *Ocenebra interfossa*, has five sharply defined whorls and reaches a length of 2.5 cm. Like all whelks this one is a carnivore which feeds on barnacles, clams, and oysters.

Sculptured Rock
Whelk

In the middle zone the Black Turban of the High Tide Zone is replaced by the Brown Turban, *Tegula brunnea*, although the two territories over lap somewhat. The Brown Turban appears only on the open coast, and is more abundant intertidally in Oregon than in British Columbia. Both species commonly give "piggy-back" rides to other snails, especially to the slipper shells.

Brown Turban

Zone IV The Low Tide Zone

It is in the Low Tide Zone that the tidepools are uncovered only a few times each month or year. This region is tremendously crowded because a greater number and variety of plants and animals live here than at all the other tide levels. Many of the animals common to the Middle Tide Zone occupy the zone too, as do others that move up from levels below low tide. Every tidepool, every rock, and every cluster of seaweed, becomes home to countless plants and animals because the region is very seldom exposed to waves, sun, and wind, and even when the tide drops almost every square centimeter is covered with protective seaweeds.

The sea urchin is a sure sign of the Low Tide Zone, and though there are both green and brown seaweeds, the red are also abundant. In fact, the Low Tide Zone is commonly called the "Red Algal Zone", but on some beaches many of the red seaweeds seem small when compared to the large brown ones.

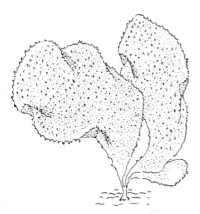

Turkish Towel

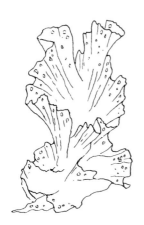

Red Laver

Take time to enjoy the colors and patterns of the seaweeds woven into a patchwork quilt of browns, reds, and purples. One of the most conspicuous is the bright red Turkish Towel, *Gigartina exasperata*, its wart-like out-growths suggesting the texture of a rough bristly towel, its one or two broad blades reaching 30 to 40 cm long. Common in the Low Tide Zone and in subtidal waters, Turkish Towel is frequently washed up on the beach, especially after winter storms, where its colors and its texture attract attention.

Sprinkled with tiny holes the beautiful thick ruffled blades of Red Laver or Dulse, *Porphyra* sp., look very much like Sea Lettuce. But Red Laver ranges from olive-green to brownish-purple, and often an oily appearance reflects the colors of the rainbow. Its single blade feels like thick stretchy rubber. Dulse is an important edible seaweed in some parts of the world: eat it raw, chew it as gum, use it as a relish, mix it with salads, or spread it like jam on crackers. Processed in a variety of ways, it is used as thickeners in soft ice cream, candy bars, and tooth paste, and as flavoring in soups and sauces.

One iridescent seaweed seems to be covered with oil and reflects all the colors of the rainbow when wet, Rainbow Seaweed, *Iridaea cordata*, its reddish blades usually quite broad and smooth and sleek and reaching a length of about 30 cm. Generally a group of blades grows from the same holdfast, but usually only one becomes large and conspicuous.

Rainbow Seaweed

Notice the bushy clumps of a dull reddish-brown or reddish-purple seaweed on the rocks and lining the tidepools, Iodine Seaweed, *Prionitis lanceolata*, up to 35 cm tall. The smooth main blade is long and narrow and flattened, 3 to 8 cm wide, and usually tapered to a point, and usually with "bladelets" of a similar shape coming from its margins. The seaweed is attached by a small disc-like holdfast. Pick it up and smell the iodine.

Iodine Seaweed

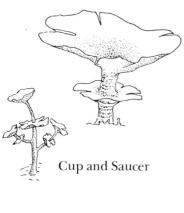

Cup and Saucer

A curious purplish-red seaweed commonly found in the lower zone, Cup and Saucer, *Constantinea simplex*, has a short thick stalk branching out into a plate-like blade. The seaweed may branch several times though the stalk continues up through each blade, the mature ones looking like several cups and saucers stacked one on top of the other. The blades of young specimens are perfectly round, but as the seaweed matures the blades tear into wedge-shaped segments. The stalk is only 2 or 3 cm long and the blades generally 5 or 6 cm wide.

A lovely rose-red seaweed attracts attention because it is perforated with numerous elliptical holes, Red Eyelet Silk, *Rhodymenia pertusa*. Usually a single blade, but sometimes numerous smaller bladelets arise near the base of the holdfast which is short and broadens into a wide round blade reaching a length of 1 meter and a width of 30 cm. Fairly common at the lowest tide levels and especially in deeper water offshore.

Red Eyelet Silk

Occasionally, in permanently submerged tide-pools there may be a strange green seaweed like soft velvet, Sea Staghorn; *Codium fragile*. From 10 to 30 cm or more in length, it is about as thick as a pencil, with branches which repeatedly fork like the antlers of a deer. The holdfast is a broad spongy disc. A long time resident of our coast, Sea Staghorn has only recently established itself on the Atlantic Coast.

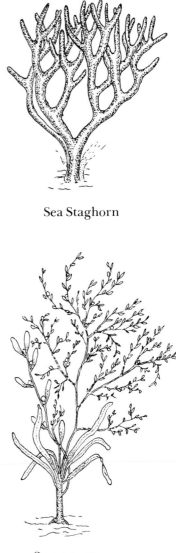

Sea Staghorn

Hanging down in tangled masses from the rocks or floating in huge beds offshore, the yellowish-brown seaweed is Sargassum, *Sargassum muticum*, a newcomer to our coast and often called "Japanese Weed". It probably came here with the Japanese Oysters in the early 1900s and is now well established, especially in quiet bays and estuaries. The seaweed has a long narrow stem that branches several times, each branch having several flattened narrow blades. Reproduction takes place in clusters of tiny round floats which are filled with gas to give the seaweed buoyancy. Large plants grow to 1 and 2 meters in length.

Sargassum

Bull Kelp

Photo 93 p. 47

When the tide drops very low on the shore, a group of conspicuous brown seaweeds come into view. These kelps — a term denoting any large brown seaweed — form a "forest" just offshore. Explore them during extreme low tides or after a fall or winter storm when unusually high waves have washed their decaying stalks and large massive holdfasts ashore. These huge seaweed tangles harbor hordes of beach hoppers and other small scavengers.

Probably the best known is Bull Kelp, *Nereocystis luetkeana*. Off almost any rocky shore there will be great beds of it, but the tides do not always fall far enough to expose the branching holdfasts. Bull Kelp is whip-like, having a long thin hollow stalk leading to a floating bulb, with several long thin blades arising from the bulb. The kelp develops in the spring and generally dies off in the succeeding winter, reaching its amazing length of up to 20 meters in only one growing season. Some live for two years.

Another easy-to-identify dark brown kelp is Split Kelp, *Laminaria setchellii*. The bottom part of the stem is rigid, but becomes flexible and widens out into a broad smooth blade usually cut into a number of thin strips. The stem reaches 1.5 meters, the blade 15 to 20 cm wide and 50 to 80 cm long. The profusely branched holdfast is very conspicuous when washed ashore.

Split Kelp

One of the most profuse kelps is the olive or rich yellow-green Sugar Kelp, *Laminaria saccharina*. The stem widens out gradually to form a long wide blade, some reaching a meter or more in length, but when that long they are generally surf-torn. Two rows of ripple marks run the length of the blade. Used as a food in Japan, and used locally as a stabilizer in instant puddings, ice creams, and candies.

Another large, easily recognized rich brown seaweed, Seersucker, *Costaria costata*, occurs low intertidally and high subtidally. It has five distinctive ribs running the length of the blade, giving it a puckered appearance, but these are raised only on one side. The size varies considerably, from 10 to 30 cm wide and from 1.5 to 3 meters or more in length. The holdfast is a short and tangled mass of wide-spreading branches.

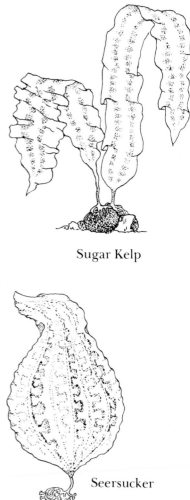

Sugar Kelp

Seersucker

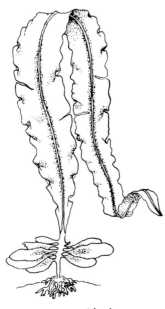

Alaria

A very common olive-green kelp forming large beds in rough waters and often washed up on the shore, Alaria, *Alaria marginata,* has a single large smooth blade with a thick conspicuous midrib. The blade is 20 to 35 cm wide, slightly wavy, and 2 to 3 meters in length. Frequently the tip of the blade is torn, and the midrib actually extends beyond it. The holdfast consists of many short solid branches, and reproduction takes place above the holdfast in the small, brown, oval bladelets, 10 to 12 cm in length.

A delicate leaf-like kelp of the lowest zone, Acid Kelp, *Desmarestia ligulata,* has thick yellowish-brown to olive-green flattened bladelets on opposite sides of the main stem. Acid Kelp is large for such a delicate-looking species, mature specimens ranging from 25 cm to 3 meters in length. The short, flat, and rigid holdfast may be 30 cm across. Specimens vary in size and shape. Younger ones have very slender branches with numerous small bladelets, giving them a more delicate feather-like appearance than mature specimens. Acid Kelp contains so much sulphuric acid in its cells that once picked the seaweed rapidly disintegrates because the acid escapes. When washed up onto shore the kelp becomes mushy, and bleached ghostly white, and when dried by the hot sun it looks and feels like crisp tissue paper.

Acid Kelp

Another attractive kelp with its fringed blades and swollen floats, the Feather Boa, *Egregia menziesii*, looks like the once-fashionable scarf made of feathers. The main branch of 5 meters or more in length is flattened and covered with numerous outgrowths which make it look and feel like rough sandpaper. At repeated intervals, smaller flattened blades arise from the main branches, up to 5 or 6 cm, and some of these blades swell to become small air bladders about the size of olives. The holdfast is repeatedly branched and may be as large as 15 to 20 cm across. Olive-green to chocolate-brown. Very common on moderately sheltered shores in the lower zones, but also slightly higher on the shore of the open coast.

Feather Boa

One very distinctive kelp forms luxuriant offshore forests on the open coast, Perennial Kelp, *Macrocystis integrifolia*, a seaweed living only in deep water with strong wave action. Perennial Kelp becomes gigantic, the largest 20 to 30 meters in length, with a holdfast as large as a clothes basket! The main stem of Perennial Kelp branches at regular intervals into shiny brown corrugated blades, each bearing pear-shaped air bladders which enable the kelp to float at the surface. The species is world-wide and perennial. Storms and high tides commonly wash it ashore and pile it into massive drifts. It grows in great beds, and in many parts of the world it is harvested with a mowing machine, towed by barge to a factory, and manufactured into algin, an amazingly versatile product used in ice cream, puddings, salad dressings, syrups, lotions, paints, polishes, insecticides, and film emulsions.

Perennial Kelp

Several different brightly colored sea stars live in the lower zones and in deep water offshore, preferring to live where they can hold onto hard rocks. Their ability to move and to cling onto rocks depends on their tube feet which are arranged in two or more series underneath each arm, and on their water-vascular system, a highly efficient network of inside plumbing. In a submerged sea star the tube feet alternately extend and contract, attaching to the substrate by suction-cup arrangements at the tips. Special muscles direct the motion of the feet, permitting the animal to move. These tube feet work as suction cups and as levers to pull and shove the body forward. Other parts of the water-vascular system — the sieve plate, the water canal, and the stone canal — are also involved in the operation of the tube feet. The function of the sieve-plate or maderporite is still unclear, but that there is much exchange of liquid through it is doubtful.

Mottled
Star
Photo 48 p. 32

A sea star very similar in size and shape to the Common Purple or Ochre Star of the higher zones, the Mottled Star, *Evasterias troschelii*, is generally dull or mottled purple, brown, or orange. The star-like pattern of white spines is like that of the Common Purple or Ochre Star, but the arms of the Mottled Star, or Slender-rayed Star, are longer and narrower in proportion to its body, and make this sea star seem more graceful. Most specimens range between 25 to 30 cm across, though some measure up to 50 cm.

A fairly abundant sea star protected by a rocky shore, the Leather Star, *Dermasterias imbricata*, has a mottled green, gray, and brownish-red upper surface and measures 20 to 25 cm across. Its five rays are firm, wide, and webbed, and the two rows of tube feet arranged in a narrow groove on the underside of each ray look like zippers. Slimy to touch, this animal feels like wet suede leather because it lacks the short spines common to most sea stars. It has a peculiar garlic smell.

Leather Star
Photo 49 p. 32

106

One rather large pale pink sea star that prefers deep water, but occasionally becomes stranded during extreme low tides, is the Pink Star, *Pisaster brevispinus*, a close relative to the smaller Common Purple or Ochre Star. Its much shorter lavender-tipped spines give this sea star a softer appearance. Pink Stars feed voraciously on sand dollars and clams, and reach a gigantic size, generally 50 to 70 cm across.

Pink Star
Photo 47 p. 31

On beaches with lots of loose rocks there is a common, but not so obvious sea star called the Six-rayed Star, *Leptasterias hexactis*. Very few other species have six rays and the Six-rayed Star is one of the smallest, reaching a maximum width of 8 to 9 cm. Generally dull gray, greenish-gray, or almost black, though occasionally some are orange or pink. Commonly called the Brooding Star because the female broods her eggs and releases the tiny sea stars only when they have developed enough to cling to the rocks.

Six-rayed Star
Photo 52 p. 32

A spectacular sea star ranging widely but most abundant on rocky shores, the Sunflower Star, *Pycnopodia helianthoides*, is bright pink, purple, or orange and is possibly the largest of the sea stars, having a spread quite commonly of 60 to 80 cm. It also has the greatest number of rays, beginning with only six and increasing with age up to twenty-four, and even more. It is also the most active of the sea stars, and can travel at about three meters a minute. The fastest sea star afoot! The underside is a mass of tube feet which, along with its great size and soft flexible body, enables the star to travel equally well over sandy, muddy, and rocky bottoms. The Sunflower Star is a feared predator. Put one into a populated tidepool, and watch the violent action as hermit crabs, limpets, abalones, and even snails, practically run to get away.

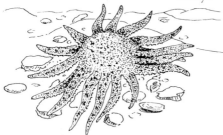

Sunflower Star
Photo 43 p. 29

Another sea star occasionally turns up during very low tides, the Sun Star, *Solaster stimpsoni*. This one travels widely, visiting rocky shores and sandy beaches. It has ten long, graceful rays, and a body somewhat gritty to the touch because of tiny spines. Usually bright orange or pink with a grayish-blue or grayish-purple line running down each ray, the Sun Star measures 20 to 50 cm across.

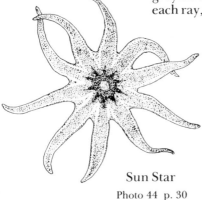

Sun Star
Photo 44 p. 30

A brilliant red or reddish-orange sea star found on rocks or hiding in crevices has the appropriate name Blood Star, *Henricia leviuscula*. Its comparatively small and graceful body is only 10 to 12 cm from the tip of one ray to the tip of the one across from it, and its five rays feel like fine sandpaper. The Blood Star, like the Brooding Star, retains its young in brood pouches around the mouth.

Blood Star
Photo 51 p. 32

Another bright red sea star, the Vermilion Star, *Mediaster aequalis*, with its wide center, grows to 17 cm from tip to tip. Easy to identify because the armor of raised calcareous plates and the row of plates along the sides of each ray create a distinctive pattern.

Vermilion Star
Photo 45 p. 30

One of the most exquisite sea stars on the Pacific Coast is the Rose Star, *Crossaster papposus*, a bright reddish-orange, generally with mottled tan patches creating concentric designs. Like the Sun Star, the Rose Star has ten narrow rays, but its body is wider and the rays not so long — width up to 12 to 15 cm tip to tip. On its top side the clusters of thorn-like spines give it a local common name, "Crown of Thorns". Though rare intertidally, very low tides occasionally uncover the Rose Star, and divers often bring them ashore where their rare beauty stirs a great excitement. Like the brightly colored Blood Star and Vermilion Star, this one often becomes a trophy decorating basements, recreation rooms, and schools. A particularly sorrowful fate for such rare species.

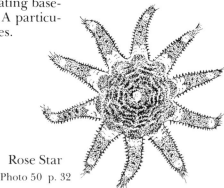

Rose Star
Photo 50 p. 32

109

When the tide falls very low it may uncover a group of strange-looking animals called sea squirts, or tunicates. They are firm "blobs" with two openings at the top, either on distinct siphons or on little bumps on the surface and named for their ability to squirt water when disturbed. Sea squirts are quite remarkable, for although they resemble sponges the young actually have a simple nerve cord and the species is related to the vertebrates. They filter microscopic food through the uppermost siphon-like opening and water and waste material flows out through the lowermost opening.

Warty Sea Squirt

One that lives in holes and crevices at the low tide line or attaches itself to pilings, the Warty Sea Squirt, *Pyura haustor*, has a wrinkled, baggy body. The dull orange-brown to reddish-brown stalk is covered with mud, sand, broken shells, gravel, and algae. When extended its bright red siphons may reach 5 or 6 cm.

A sea squirt living on the protected sides of rocks on the open coast is the Stalked Sea Squirt, *Styela montereyensis*. Easy to see and recognize: dark red or yellowish-brown in color and shaped like a rose vase. The stalk reaches a height of 8 to 12 cm, and its many longish grooves taper top to bottom.

Stalked Sea Squirt
Photo 60 p. 36

The Red Sea Squirt, *Cnemidocarpa finmarkiensis*, is red or pinkish-red and extraordinarily beautiful, especially when its bright red siphons are extended. The crater-like siphons are quite round when the animal is left alone, but when disturbed they close down to form a small cross. A large specimen can be about 2.5 cm in height.

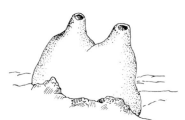

Red Sea Squirt
Photo 62 p. 36

Another sea squirt found on rocky shores exposed to heavy wave action, Sea Pork, *Aplidium californicum*, is a colonial sea squirt forming peculiar irregular masses which may be 1 to 2 cm in thickness and may look like a pancake. Highly variable in color, going from white or pale reddish-brown to brownish-yellow. When growing over an irregular shape, such as a barnacle, the Sea Pork looks like a leg of pork.

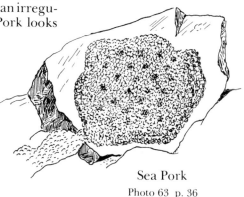

Sea Pork
Photo 63 p. 36

In this lower zone a variety of other chitons outnumber the Black Chiton. In fact, on our own West Coast chitons are at their best: they are larger, more abundant, and more conspicuous than anywhere else in the world. Chitons have strange-looking armored bodies and poorly developed sense organs; they have neither eyes nor tentacles, but many microscopic bumps scattered on the body, most of the smallest bumps sensitive to touch, and the others sensitive to light. Chitons cannot see, but can tell light from dark. During high tide, or at night, they wander out to scrape the rocks for algae, but never wander very far, always returning to the same spot.

Two fairly common species of chitons on our coast, the "mossy chitons" have bristles, or hairs, on a gristle-like girdle that runs around the margin of the body. Well camouflaged, they live in crevices, tidepools, and on the rocks under seaweeds. The most conspicuous, the common Mossy Chiton, *Mopalia muscosa*, has a stiff, thick bristly girdle and is likely to have plants and animals growing on its plates. The other, the Hairy Chiton, *Mopalia lignosa*, has rather soft hairs, is dull green or brown, and occasionally has yellow tinges on the plates. Both species grow to 8 or 10 cm in length.

Mossy Chiton

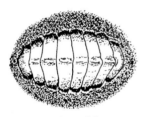

Hairy Chiton

Photo 27 p. 25

Look on or near coralline algae for a creature called the Lined Chiton, *Tonicella lineata*, about 5 cm in length and 2.5 cm wide, with a smooth shiny surface marked by brown lines that zigzag across a field of gold, pink, and lavender-blue or green. This chiton feeds on the pinkish coralline algae and, of course, on the tiny organisms clinging to that algae.

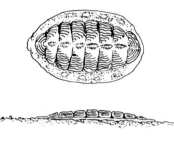

Lined Chiton
Photo 29 p. 25

The largest chiton in the world lives on our own coast, the Gum Boot Chiton, *Cryptochiton stelleri*. It reaches 25 cm or more, its color and texture almost that of the reddish-brown sole of a rubber boot. The light bony plates are not visible because a very tough rough gritty and leathery girdle completely overgrows them. The large creeping foot adheres tightly to rocks. Gently slip a wide-edged putty knife beneath the foot to pry it off. But if the animal is wedged tightly, damage is likely to occur, so leave it alone!

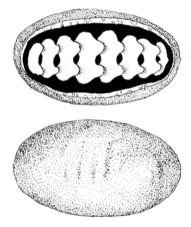

Gum Boot Chiton
Photo 30 p. 25

Blue Top Shell

Photo 18 p. 21

A strikingly beautiful snail on the protected outer coast and in sheltered bays, the Blue Top Shell, *Calliostoma ligatum*, grows to a height and width of slightly greater than 2 cm, its seven whorls set with many spiralling raised ridges. Brick-red or brownish, sometimes almost blue; on a worn shell the blue layer underneath is more evident. Blue Top Shells graze on seaweeds and on the thin film of greenish-brown algae covering the rocks.

Pearly Top Shell

Another top-shaped snail on sheltered rocky shores, the Pearly Top Shell, *Lirularia lirulata*, has a shell wider than it is tall with about five whorls with nearly smooth, alternating ridges. Smaller than the Blue Top Shell, about 1 cm in height, the Pearly Top is pinkish-brown or pinkish-purple with a silvery sheen, and has a little hole near the center of the base. In some countries people polish various pearly shells and use them as jewelry. Though several species live on our coast, this one is the most widely distributed.

Still another is the exquisite Opalescent Top Shell, *Calliostoma annulatum*, about 3 cm in height, the yellowish or brownish-orange shell almost a perfect cone with eight flattened whorls, each ornamented with a spiralling beaded purple band. The body of the snail itself is an unusually bright salmon color sprinkled with rich brown specks. Though uncommon intertidally, the Opalescent Top Shell lives in deep water and occasionally comes into sheltered kelp and eelgrass flats at the low tide line.

Opalescent Top Shell

Photo 17 p. 21

A fairly common snail on rock and cobble beaches, the Wrinkled Amphissa, *Amphissa columbiana*, grows to about 2 or 3 cm in height. Its six or seven whorls appear to be wrinkled because the fine thread-like spiralling ridges are intersected by many prominent lengthwise ridges. The shells of young specimens are generally thin and fragile, those of older specimens thicker and likely covered with an encrusting growth. The color varies considerably, but browns and oranges are most common. The Wrinkled Amphissa belongs to a rather large group of small snails collectively called "dove shells", and characterized by long slender shells tapering to a sharp point. They are seldom-seen scavengers feeding on soft algae and dead animal matter, and finding food and shelter under rocks and seaweeds.

Wrinkled Amphissa

Photo 15 p. 21

Hooked Slipper
Shell

The slipper shells are a treat to find. Such odd little snails! Their limpet-like shells somewhat resemble a slipper, especially when the snail has died and only the shell remains. Like clams, slipper snails are filter feeders. They cling to rocks and to the shells of other snails, especially of Top Shells and Turban Shells.

Most common intertidally is the Hooked Slipper Shell, *Crepidula adunca*, with its apex particularly obvious and sharply arched or "hooked". Brown on the outside, white on the inside, the largest specimens are only about 2 cm long.

White Slipper Shell

The White Slipper Shell, *Crepidula nummaria*, may be long and narrow, or nearly circular; it may be thick, or it may be thin and delicate. However, its shell is only slightly arched, and not very high. Generally, the shell is white and reaches a length of 3 or 4 cm.

Another intertidal slipper shell, the Wrinkled Slipper Shell, *Crepidula lingulata*, has an irregular, or wrinkled, low white shell and reaches a length of 2.5 cm. Like the other slipper shells, these tiny empty shells wash ashore, or decorate the bottoms of tidepools, or contribute to the mosaic of broken shell and other debris at the high tide line.

Several species of horn snails appear on our coast, but the one most likely to be intertidal is the Threaded Horn Snail, *Bittium eschrichtii*, its long, slender "drill" shaped shell a very popular mobile home for hermit crabs. About nine dull brown or grayish-brown whorls gradually taper to a point. When fully grown this scavenger feeds on the film of algae on the rocks, and on seaweeds, especially on eelgrass, and is 1 or 2 cm long.

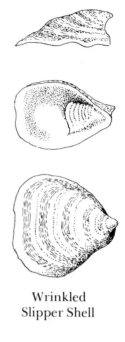

Wrinkled
Slipper Shell

Threaded Horn Snail

Leafy Hornmouth

Photo 19 p. 21

A richly ornamented snail found in surf-swept areas receiving some shelter is the Leafy Hornmouth, *Ceratostoma foliatum*, commonly 6 to 8 cm long. It has extensive frills, like three thin "wings", arising from a shell of six or seven grayish-white or brownish whorls. The Leafy Hornmouth is an active carnivorous snail which feeds on large barnacles and on other snails, using its radula to pierce a hole through the victim's shell and remove the meat. In the early summer it deposits its egg cases on moist rocks or on its own shell.

One of the largest snails on the Pacific Coast, the Hairy Triton, *Fusitriton oregonensis*, has a handsome shell reaching a length of 10 cm, its 6 or 7 very distinct rounded whorls covered with brown bristles or hairs. The egg case clusters look like ears of corn, each egg case looking like a kernel, and each containing several hundred eggs. The first snails to hatch eat some of the rest of the eggs in the case.

Oregon Hairy Triton

Photo 22 p. 22

A group of odd bivalves resembling clams and oysters, but in no way related to them, are the Brachiopods, *Terebratalia transversa*, their two calcareous shells only 2 or 3 cm across, an upper and lower held together by a muscle. The shells may be strongly ribbed or quite smooth: the upper shell, the larger, has an opening through which a tough retractable stem emerges and attaches to rocks. Brachiopods are generally uncommon intertidally, but may be seen occasionally during very low tides. They open their shells and trap minute food particles in water currents. Commonly called "Lamp Shells" because of their resemblance to Aladdin's lamp.

Grazing in the lowest regions of the zone is the Northern Abalone, *Haliotis kamtschatkana*, its shell flattened and wavy, one edge thin, the other thick. The shells of larger specimens may reach a length of about 12 cm. A series of holes function in the same way as the single hole in a Keyhole Limpet: water passing through the body leaves through the holes, carrying away wastes from the digestive system. Like the limpets and chitons, abalones are herbivores which graze on seaweeds and the thin film of algae covering the rocks. When dislodged from its rocky support the abalone tends to curl the edges of its broad, muscular foot. Abalones are such a seafood delicacy that shore enthusiasts and skin divers have taken so many that they now occur subtidally and only in remote areas.

Brachiopod

Northern Abalone
Photo 24 p. 23

Keyhole Limpet

One of the few limpets likely to occur in the Low Tide Zone, the Keyhole Limpet, *Diodora aspera*, has an attractive shell, usually gray or grayish-brown, sometimes with white and brown bands running down from the top. The shell is frequently covered with seaweeds and small colonial animals which make it inconspicuous. Like "true limpets" this one is a herbivore which grazes on algae. Large specimens will reach 4 or 5 cm.

Examine the underside of the Keyhole Limpet to see an interesting little worm often tucked snugly away between the foot and the shell. Called a Commensal Scaleworm, *Arctonoë vittata*, the worm curls around the limpet so completely that the two ends of the worm almost meet. The milk-white or pale yellow scaleworm matches the color of the limpet's foot. The relationship between the worm and the limpet is called a commensal relationship; marine biologists believe that the relationship is of benefit to both partners, though biologists are themselves not quite sure how. Not only might the worm benefit by a protective dwelling place, but it may partake of the limpet's own food. Just how the limpet might benefit by this apparent free-loading is unclear, but one account describes the worm as biting at the encroaching tube feet of sea star predators. Look for other species of scaleworms on many of the sea stars and especially on the Gum Boot Chiton.

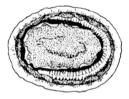

Commensal Scaleworm

On or near the pinkish coralline algae that encrust the rocks at the low tide line look for an exceptionally tall White Cap Limpet, *Acmaea mitra*. Its shell is thick and white, but appears to be almost reddish-pink because it is generally covered with the coralline algae on which the limpet feeds almost exclusively. This species is the tallest of our limpets, the height of the shell a little more than 3 cm, its tall cone shape inspiring the nickname Dunce Cap Limpet. This striking animal lives mostly in the low intertidal area, but empty shells often wash ashore.

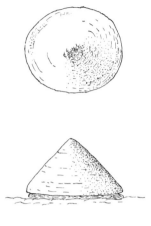

Although abundant in the higher zones, barnacles are rare in the Low Tide Zone, the commonest this low on the beach being the Thatched Barnacle, the same form that occurs higher up. The second commonest, probably the largest in the world, the Giant Acorn Barnacle, *Balanus nubilus*, may have a shell 5 to 8 cm in diameter and 10 to 12 cm in height. Young specimens have well developed thatch-like ribs, but because of erosion older ones have smoother shells. The shell is dirty white with cinnamon on the interior of the cover plates and bright purple or red patches usually near the top. Large clusters of individual Giant Acorn Barnacles often grow one upon another and though uncommon intertidally, they are abundant in deeper water and occasionally drift ashore, perhaps after being broken loose by storms.

White Cap Limpet
Photo 20 p. 21

Giant Acorn Barnacle
Photo 1 p. 17

On gravelly bottoms and places where broken shells have piled together a group of interesting bivalve animals called scallops have fan-shaped shells that have alternating furrows and ridges, similar to the familiar Shell Oil sign. They have a striking fringe of bright blue eyes surrounding the edge of the shell, each eye with double retinas and a focusing lens, and though scallops may be incapable of seeing real images, they can detect nearby shadows and nearby movements. They normally lie on the bottom with the two valves slightly open to allow the animal inside to bring in water and filter microscopic food from it. Most scallops swim by clapping their valves together and forcing water out through the opening on either side of the hinge, though other scallops are permanently attached to rocks.

Pink Scallop

Photo 26 p. 24

The shell of the Pink Scallop, *Chlamys hericia*, has unequal wing-like "ears" projecting from the hinge. Both valves have twenty-four ribs with broad pink and white bands radiating outward, like a fan. The surface feels rough because of a covering of little curved spines. This scallop reaches a length of about 6 cm, is a rapid swimmer, quick to take alarm, and commonly called the Swimming Scallop.

The Weathervane Scallop, *Pecten caurinus*, is a huge, free-swimmer with a thin, circular shell that may be 20 cm in diameter, white or brown on the outside and glossy or dull white on the inside. The right valve, on which the scallop lies, is heavily indented with twenty broad flat-topped ribs. Both the Pink Scallop and the Weathervane Scallop occur in beds on muddy or sandy bottoms in deep water offshore, and their empty shells frequently wash ashore.

Weathervane Scallop

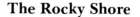

A scallop that is free-swimming until it reaches a diameter of 2 or 3 cm and thereafter attaches itself permanently to rocks is the impressive Rock Scallop, *Hinnites giganteus*. Its heavy thick shell is strongly ribbed, the outside brownish, but encrusting sponges and coralline algaes add various colors. Adult shells are often pitted with holes and badly misshapen because of boring sponges. Both shells are brownish-green on the outside, white on the inside, and have a deep purple blotch in the hinge area. Large specimens grow to 20 to 25 cm in length; 15 cm however is more common. The muscle of a Rock Scallop is particularly large and is a major food delicacy; the species is therefore now found only subtidally, except in remote areas.

Rock Scallop

Another bivalve shellfish occurring sporadically in sheltered bays as well as on the open coast, the Jingle Shell Oyster, *Pododesmus macroschisma*, has a nearly round shell generally reaching 8 cm across. If the animal attaches itself to an irregularly shaped object the shells follow the shape of that object. The lower shell is smaller and thinner than the upper, and has a notched hole through which the byssus threads pass and attach the animal to rocks. The edible flesh is bright orange. Fill your pocket with dried shells and listen to the "jingle".

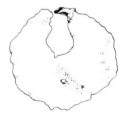

Jingle Shell Oyster

In dark moist places, under ledges, under the protected sides of rocks, and lining tidepools, orange-red cups sparkle like jewels, the Cup Corals, *Balanophyllia elegans*, really true corals, related to sea anemones, with hard cup-shaped calcareous shells supporting the body. The cup is up to 1 cm in height and in width, and built up so that the animal can draw into it when disturbed. In a living animal a series of nearly transparent tentacles surround the small mouth in the center of the cup and an incomplete gut connects with the mouth. It feeds on tiny animals trapped by the tentacles. When it dies, only the bony, chalk-white skeleton remains.

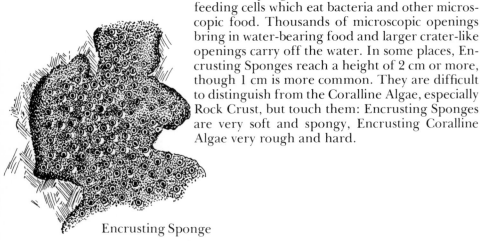

Cup Coral

Photo 65 & 66 p. 37

On the protected sides of rocks and on the undersides of moist ledges look for brightly colored, spongy carpets — greens, purples, golds, reds, and grays. Generally irregular in shape, they measure up to 10 to 30 cm across. If the growths feel soft and velvety or gelatinous they are likely one of several species of Encrusting Sponge, Phylum Porifera. Sponges are colonial animals that have feeding cells which eat bacteria and other microscopic food. Thousands of microscopic openings bring in water-bearing food and larger crater-like openings carry off the water. In some places, Encrusting Sponges reach a height of 2 cm or more, though 1 cm is more common. They are difficult to distinguish from the Coralline Algae, especially Rock Crust, but touch them: Encrusting Sponges are very soft and spongy, Encrusting Coralline Algae very rough and hard.

Encrusting Sponge

Photo 66 p. 37

Several different species of fern-like hydroids attach themselves to hard surfaces, to rocks, kelps, pilings, and to the hard shells of animals. Though hydroids may look like plants they are actually a whole colony of tiny polyps all joined together and sharing a common digestive system. They are primitive colonial animals related to sea anemones, jellyfishes, corals, and sea pens. Like their relatives, the hydroids have stinging cells which explode upon contact with tiny prey and the minute tentacles pass the paralyzed animal to the mouth.

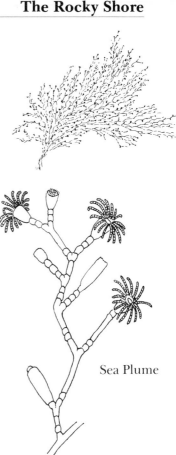

One common hydroid hangs down like delicate fuzz from pilings and rocks, the Sea Plume, *Obelia* sp. The whitish or grayish-brown thread-like stems, about 2 cm long, branch several times. The swollen reproductive organs rise from the main stem and produce free-swimming hydroid medusae which in turn individually produce eggs or sperm; the fertilized eggs develop into motile larvae which later settle and grow into new hydroid colonies.

Sea Plume

One of the larger and more distinct hydroids has delicate feather-like fronds, the Ostrich Plume Hydroid, *Aglaophenia* sp., its stiff branches forming bushy growths up to 8 to 12 cm long. Along one side of each branch are individual feeding polyps; along some branches there may be basket-like structures which contain the reproductive polyps which generally produce very small and short-lived larvae that become other hydroid colonies.

Ostrich Plume Hydroid

Photo 64 p. 37

125

Explore the massive beds of seaweeds covering the lower zones where the moist undergrowth provides shelter for a large variety of shrimp, spider crabs, and nudibranchs. Inspect their branching holdfasts for a variety of worms, and small crabs, and brittle stars.

Among the many interesting spider crabs inhabiting the massive seaweed beds is the well camouflaged Decorator Crab, *Oregonia gracilis*: it actually picks up bits and pieces of seaweeds and other materials and glues them to its body with a sticky substance from its mouth. The triangular carapace is 4 to 6 cm wide, the legs are extremely long and thin, the first ones specially constructed for handling seaweed. The rough and bristly carapace and legs allow seaweeds and colonies of small hydroids and bryozoans to settle and grow.

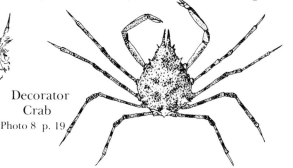

Decorator
Crab
Photo 8 p. 19

A strong aggressive spider crab, rather large with a carapace of almost 10 cm in length, frequently clings to the stems and fronds of kelps and eelgrass, the Kelp Crab, *Pugettia producta*. An olive-brown blending perfectly with the seaweeds, it has sharp spines on its carapace, and long slim legs. Unlike the sluggish Decorator, this agile crab keeps a smooth, clean body. The Kelp Crab constantly squirms when handled: his spines and pinchers are sharp: leave large specimens alone.

Kelp Crab

An interesting spider crab in kelp and eelgrass beds, the extremely hairy Helmet Crab, *Telmessus cheiragonus*, also dresses itself with seaweeds. This one has six sharp points on each side of its carapace, some about 6 cm wide. Young specimens are greenish, but adults show red, orange, or brown. These slow-moving scavengers feed on seaweeds.

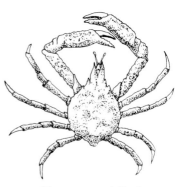

Helmet Crab

Another spider crab in kelp and eelgrass, the Sharp-nosed Crab, *Scyra acutifrons*, measures 3 to 4 cm across the carapace. Shaped much like the Decorator Crab, but with shorter and fatter legs, and a longer "nose". This slow mover, also called the Masking Crab, encourages algae and small colonizing animals to grow on its roughened body surface — sponges, bryozoans, and sea squirts. It blends into its surroundings, possibly to hide from enemies.

Sharp-nosed Crab

Photo 9 p. 19

The Hairy Crab, *Hapalogaster mertensii*, has a red or brown body covered with golden brown bristles and hairs, adults measuring up to 3 cm across the carapace. Like their distant relatives, the Hermit Crabs, Hairy Crabs have soft and slightly turned abdomens, but long ago gave up snail shells, and like the spider crabs they are walking gardens of seaweed.

Hairy Crab

Under the massive protective curtains of seaweeds or on submerged pilings or in tidepools lives a brightly colored group of delicate, soft-bodied animals called nudibranchs. Indeed they are naked, having no hard outer shell, but they do have branched gills. Also known as "sea slugs", possibly because some look like shell-less land slugs. Oddly, nudibranchs have few predators; fish will spit them out. Even the more brightly colored ones are safe, because they possibly give off unpleasant odors or are unpleasant to the taste. Other nudibranchs blend perfectly with their surroundings.

There are two broad groups of nudibranchs. The particularly beautiful aeolids are covered with finger-like gills, "cerata", that look like ornaments — the Opalescent and Frosted Nudibranchs. The others belong to the second group, the dorids, with flattened plump bodies, a rough surface much like a lemon, and gills located in a ring on the back — the Sea Lemon and the White Nudibranch. Both groups have a pair of elaborate projections, or "rhinophores" on the upper surface of the head.

Opalescent Nudibranch
Photo 34 p. 26

The most obvious nudibranch on rocky shores and in eelgrass, the little Opalescent Nudibranch, *Hermissenda crassicornis*, is about 4 cm long and adorned with reddish-brown cerata with white tips. A clear iridescent blue line like a neon light decorates each side. This species feeds on hydroids, sea squirts, and different kinds of eggs.

Another very graceful nudibranch is less common intertidally, the Frosted Nudibranch, *Dirona albolineata*, reaching 6 or 7 cm. A whitish body with some gray or brown spots; the numerous gills almost transparent, but outlined by a bright white opaque border. Feeds on sea anemones, snails, sea squirts, and bryozoans.

Frosted Nudibranch
Photo 31 p. 26

One of the largest and most conspicuous nudibranchs commonly occurs on moist rocks, in tide pools, and on pilings: the Sea Lemon, *Archidoris montereyensis*, a plump animal colored and shaped like a slice of lemon, the bumpy bright yellow skin frequently sprinkled with black peppery dots. The Sea Lemon has two thick horn-like rhinophores to the front, and six branched gills to the rear. During the summer it deposits long ribbon-like pale yellow egg masses on the moist sides of rocks, each egg mass containing thousands of minute eggs. Sea Lemons feed almost exclusively on sponges, and grow to a length of 12 cm, though 6 or 7 cm is most common.

Sea Lemon
Photo 32 p. 26

Two absolutely white nudibranchs occur in similar locations. The first, the White Nudibranch, *Archidoris odhneri*, looks something like a Sea Lemon, but is slightly shorter, about 5 or 6 cm, much plumper, and covered with slightly raised and rounded bumps. The second, the White Nudibranch, *Adalaria* sp., photo 41 p. 28, is 3 to 4 cm long, less plump, and covered with elongated nodules. Both species feed on sponges.

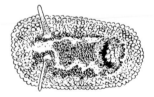

White Nudibranch
Archidoris odhneri

A small brown nudibranch feeds on bryozans among seaweeds and in mussel beds and on the undersides of moist rocks, the Brown Nudibranch, *Acanthodoris brunnea*, about 2.5 cm long. Rich brown with irregular black splotches, it has tiny yellow or white specks over the body. At the rear, seven brown and yellow gill plumes; to the front, two long black rhinophores. Like the Sea Lemon and the White Nudibranch, the body of this one has a rough, warty appearance because the surface is thickly set with rounded bumps. During the spring and summer, turn over loose rocks near the Low Tide Zone to see their white egg ribbons which adhere to the undersides of rocks.

Brown Nudibranch

129

Ringed Nudibranch

Photo 37 p. 26

Another nudibranch, often called the Ringed Nudibranch, *Diaulula sandiegensis*, lives under ledges and rocks and seaweeds. Easy to recognize because of its light brown to grayish-white body covered with numerous reddish or brownish spots or rings of various sizes. A good example of an animal with several common names (Spotted Nudibranch, Ringed Nudibranch, Brown-spotted Nudibranch, Leopard Nudibranch) it reaches a length of 6 or 7 cm and a width of 2 or 3 cm. A carnivore also feeding on sponges.

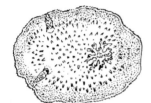

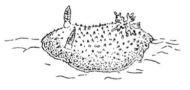

Very striking but somewhat uncommon, the Yellow-edged Nudibranch, *Cadlina luteomarginata*, is pure white with bright lemon trimmings around the edges. Carnivorous, it feeds on sponges and grows to 4 or 5 cm.

Yellow-edged Nudibranch

Photo 38 p. 26

One of the most beautiful of the species is our Orange-spotted Nudibranch, *Triopha carpenteri*, its colors so brilliant that the animal seems unreal — bright spots of orange on a pure white body and gills. Rather large and sausage-shaped, it ranges in length from 6 to 12 cm and feeds on small colonial animals like bryozoans.

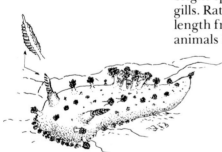

Orange-spotted Nudibranch

Photo 39 p. 27

Bright red and difficult to see because it blends perfectly with the patches of red sponge on which it feeds, the Red Nudibranch, *Rostanga pulchra*, is rarely larger than 1 or 2 cm. Its comparatively small elliptical body is rounded in front and pointed to the rear: near the front, two short stout tentacles; to the rear, ten or twelve branched gills that can completely retract into the sheath. In spring or early summer, look closely to see the coiled egg masses which are the same red color of the sponges.

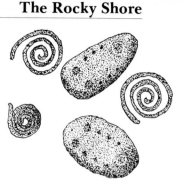

Red Nudibranch
Photo 35 p. 26

Inspect the hard, crusty patches of bryozoans for the Cryptic Nudibranch, *Doridella steinbergae*, a small flat nearly transparent nudibranch of only 1 or 1.5 cm. Perfectly camouflaged, its white and brown pattern matches the box-like houses of the bryozoans on which it feeds exclusively.

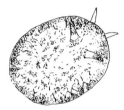

Cryptic Nudibranch
Photo 42 p. 28

On the fronds and stems of outer tidepool kelps and on rocks in the lower zones, thin hard crusty Bryozoans, *Eurystomella* sp., grow in patches shaped like the intricate designs on frosty window panes. Each patch is actually a colony of several hundred small animals, each one living in a box-like house; the arrangement of these boxes gives the colonies their beauty and texture. Because some may cover several square centimeters and seem to be mats of moss, Bryozoans are commonly called "moss animals". There are several different species, each one of a different color, shape, and texture.

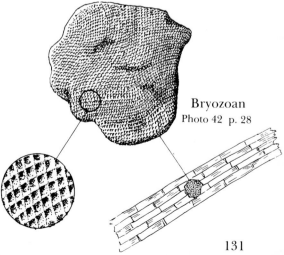

Bryozoan
Photo 42 p. 28

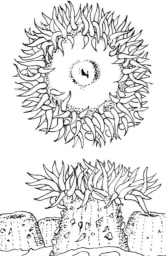

Several large species of beautifully colored sea anemones live in the larger tidepools and in sheltered rock crevices, especially on the open coast. Spend a few minutes trying to feed them: if hungry most anemones will take anything offered: small fish, crabs, or snails. The tiny stinging capsules at the tip of the tentacles trap and paralyze prey, but are usually harmless to humans. The anemone swallows the victim whole and digests it, then spits out the indigestible bits and pieces of shell, and expands back into its innocent-looking flower-like posture.

Giant Green Anemone
#73 p. 41 & #84 p. 46

The Giant Green Anemone, *Anthopleura xanthogrammica*, is great of size and a thrill to see. This giant can be 25 to 30 cm wide when fully open, but can contract to nearly half that size. It prefers to live alone, or spaced evenly in tidepools, and supports large populations of microscopic green algae which give it the bright green color. They are commonly covered with pieces of shell and gravel: some biologists think the cover reflects sunlight, holds in moisture, and cools the animal when the tide drops.

**Red and Green
Anemone**

Photo 68 & Photo 69 p. 39

One handsome sea anemone typically occurs in tidepools or partially buried in gravel, the Red and Green Anemone, *Tealia crassicornis*, about the same size as the Giant Green Anemone, but with thicker tentacles. The central oral disk is usually colored a dull greenish-gray, but the tentacles have lighter cross bands and perhaps pink or reddish streaks. The column is usually light olive-green streaked with brilliant red, but is sometimes completely red.

A sea anemone that is rarely exposed because it occurs subtidally or hides away in protected places under ledges and in caves where there is little wave action, the Plumose Anemone, *Metridium senile*, is an exceptionally long one reaching 50 to 60 cm when extended. This "sea flower" is most impressive at high tide when, under water, it expands fully to reveal its feathery snowy-white or orange tentacles. But when the tide drops the anemone hangs down, unattractively, from ledges, dock pilings, and floats.

Plumose Anemone

Photo 72 p. 41

An unusual sea anemone living on the blades of eelgrass and attaching to rocks at the bottom of tidepools, the Brooding Sea Anemone, *Epiactis prolifera*, may be green, red, or brown with darker colored stripes and only 2 cm at the base of the column. The young become motile within the parent, escape through the mouth, slide down the column, and attach themselves to the base of the column of the parent anemone; when about 5 mm high they leave the parent to begin life on their own.

Brooding Sea Anemone

Photo 74 p. 41

133

Green Sea Urchin

Photo 54 p. 33

Huge herds of sea urchins graze in the larger tidepools or on the bottom offshore. These sea "porcupines" have long tube feet, and bristling spines on ball and socket joints which give a surprising range of movement. Sea urchins have five moveable jaws, or teeth, called "Aristotle's Lantern" because the Greek philosopher and naturalist described the structure as being similar to an ancient lamp. These teeth come together as a powerful feeding mechanism. Sea urchins feed mostly on seaweeds, especially kelp, and sometimes destroy whole kelp forests by cutting away at the lower portions of the plant. Look for the brittle white "shell", or test, of sea urchins, and examine the five-point star pattern, a clue to the close relationship of sea urchins to sea stars.

One dull green or yellow-green sea urchin that occurs widely in tidepools and on rocks not exposed to the full force of breaking waves is the Green Sea Urchin, *Strongylocentrotus droebachiensis*. The shell is comparatively small, reaching a width of 8 cm; the short blunt spines crowd close together and are 1 to 3 cm long.

The largest on our coast, the Red Sea Urchin, *Strongylocentrotus franciscanus*, also lives in semi-sheltered waters. Its hard outer shell may be 12 to 14 cm across and its long sharp spines may reach 5 to 8 cm. Colors range from pink to deep red to purple, though red is most common. Occasionally large aggregations form thick prickly mats on the bottom of tidepools at low tide level and in deeper waters offshore.

Red Sea Urchin

Photo 56 p. 33

A surf-loving urchin preferring the open coast is the Purple Sea Urchin, *Strongylocentrotus purpuratus*, a distinct deep reddish-purple, its outer shell reaching 8 cm in diameter. The dense and fairly short spines reach 2 to 3 cm. On softer rocks it sometimes works itself into a hollow that almost completely entombs the animal and in some places, where wave shock is great, the soft bedrock is a honeycomb of great herds of them.

Purple Sea Urchin
Photo 55 p. 33

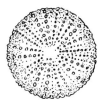 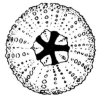

Once in a while a little octopus becomes stranded in a pool of water at low tide. Chances are this baby is of the largest species found anywhere, the Pacific Octopus, *Octopus dofleini*. A full grown specimen may weigh about 45 kg (100 pounds) and have an armspread of 4 to 6 meters. Octopuses are weird-looking animals with a warty, bag-shaped body, yellow eyes that stand out like doorknobs, and eight arms covered with suction cups — so weird-looking that man has for centuries feared the sight of them and called them "devilfish". An unfortunate reputation: octopuses are really quite shy, often living alone in dark caves, under rocks, and in old shipwrecks. Their favorite food is crabs, but they also eat snails, oysters, abalones, clams, mussels, and small fish.

Pacific Octopus
Photo 83 p. 45

Adhering to the sides of rocks and particularly lining tidepools are several different species of highly specialized tube worms, their tube providing protection for the worm while the tentacles trap microscopic food and pass it down to the mouth. Tube worms are related to other segmented worms, like the pile worm and the earthworm. They are well adapted for their tube-dwelling life. For example, their tentacles are so sensitive to light that a shadow passing over the pool causes the tentacles to withdraw instantly; wait a few minutes and the tentacles will once more emerge and the animal will begin to feed again.

One of the largest and most beautiful of our tube worms, the Calcareous Tube Worm, *Serpula vermicularis*, has a coiled or rambling hard white tube, long feathery tentacles, and segmented body. The tentacles are generally bright red with fine white stripes. The size is variable, but the tubes of large specimens may be 15 to 20 cm long and about as wide as a thick crayon, though the worm inside the tube may not be much more than 6 to 8 cm long.

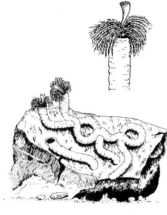

Calcareous Tube Worm
Photo 94 p. 48

Another tube worm decorates tidepools and pilings, the Feather Duster Worm, *Schizobranchia insignis*, large clumps of many small individual tubes. The leathery, parchment-like material enclosing the individual worm is more flexible than that of the Calcareous Tube Worm. Red, orange, brown, gray, or greenish, the tentacles fork several times and look like feathers. When submerged, the plumes are expanded and the mass resembles a luxuriant bouquet of colorful feather dusters. In places the tangled tubes of Feather Duster Worms form such great masses that they provide dense underwater cities in which smaller organisms live.

Feather Duster Worm

While exploring the tidepools, chase after the fairy-like shrimp. This marvelous animal darts forwards and backwards and manoeuvers loops with ease, all the while propelling itself with its swimming legs, called swimmerettes, and by a sudden flick of its tail. Catch one if you can.

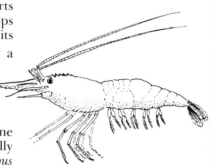

Broken-back Shrimp

There are many species of shrimps, but the one most common intertidally on rocky and gravelly bottoms is the Broken-back Shrimp, *Heptacarpus* sp., conspicuous because of a sharp bend in its back. Though the body is generally transparent it will show a slight green, gray, brown, or reddish tinge to enable it to blend in with the background.

Another common shrimp around dock pilings and floats or in sand or gravelly bottoms where there is a rapid current, the Coon-striped Shrimp, *Pandalus danae*, is named after the racoon because of its grayish-brown, red, and white markings. The adult Broken-back and adult Coon-striped live in deep water, but the juveniles — and the occasional adult — may be found in tidepools, in shallow water, or in seaweeds during low tides. The young may be only 3 or 4 cm in length, but mature specimens may reach more than 15 cm. A favorite in our fish markets.

Coon-striped Shrimp

In crevices and between rocks, watch for the brightly colored tentacles of a group of bizarre-looking creatures called sea cucumbers. Dig gently around the animal to find the crown of tentacles attached to a rather long leathery body looking something like a dill pickle. The radial symmetry of sea cucumbers indicates that they are closely related to sea urchins and sea stars: the cucumbers have five regions running the length of the body similar to the five point pattern of sea stars and sea urchins.

A cucumber found frequently in large numbers in the middle and lower zones, the Orange Sea Cucumber, *Cucumaria miniata*, is reddish-orange or purplish-brown, with bright orange or reddish tentacles. It is difficult to dislodge because the tube feet attach firmly to surrounding objects. If undisturbed the animal may extend to its full 20 cm, but when annoyed contracts and becomes smaller and very firm.

Orange Sea Cucumber

Another cucumber creeps under rocks at the low tide line, the White Sea Cucumber, *Eupentacta quinquesemita*, known for its bristly appearance caused by five sets of longish double rows of tube feet. It is fairly small for a cucumber, reaching a maximum length of only 8 or 9 cm. Color ranges from nearly white to pale yellow. The White Sea Cucumber is not so common as the Orange Sea Cucumber, because the White prefers quieter waters and lives so far down that it is practically a subtidal species.

White Sea Cucumber

Photo 58 p. 34

The Armored Sea Cucumber, *Psolus chitonoides*, is an intriguing creature, uncommon intertidally, but living in deeper water and clinging tightly to rocks or very slowly creeping along. It is so odd that people often do not recognize it as a sea cucumber; in fact, it more closely resembles a chiton. Note the species name *chitonoides*: the upper surface is covered with hard, overlapping calcareous plates. Unlike most sea cucumbers the body appears to be cut lengthwise, like a dill pickle cut in half; the side with the three rows of tube feet is perfectly flat. Beside other sea cucumbers, it is quite small, generally reaching a length of only 5 cm.

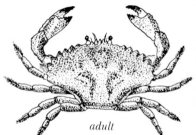

Armored
Sea Cucumber
Photo 57 p. 34

In quiet boulder-strewn bays, turn over loose rocks to uncover several species of crabs. One common crab restricted to rocky shores, the fairly large and common Red Rock Crab, *Cancer productus*, measures about 15 cm across the carapace. The adults are generally a solid deep red or brownish-red, while the juveniles may be streaked or mottled; the pinchers are tipped with black. At night watch this crab stalking about in tidepools searching for food. Red Rock Crabs are edible, but are not plentiful enough or large enough to be sold on the market.

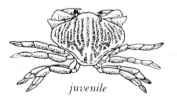

adult

juvenile

Red Rock Crab
Photo 7 p. 18

Under rocks, especially where mud and gravel has collected, lives the little Black-clawed Crab, *Lophopanopeus bellus*. This species looks something like the Purple Shore Crab, but has a heavier body and has powerful claws tipped with black. The body color varies from red, to brown, to gray, to almost white, and the carapace is rarely wider than 2.5 cm. Pick one up: it will act as though it is dead and remain motionless even long after it is released.

Black-clawed Crab

On protected beaches, under loose rocks resting on fine gravel, look for an interesting small crab called the Porcelain Crab, *Petrolisthes eriomerus*, its drab olive-brown or reddish-purple body, rounded and flattened, measuring about 2 cm across. Like the hermit crabs, they have only four pairs of walking legs; "true crabs" have five. The claws are very large and smooth and extremely flat. If one of the over-sized legs becomes pinned down, the crab simply snaps off the porcelain-brittle leg and walks away, and develops a new one within a few weeks.

Porcelain Crab

The little Oregon Rock Crab, *Cancer oregonensis*, snuggles tightly into holes between and under rocks. Though similar in appearance to the Red Rock Crab, it is much smaller, only about 4 cm across, and the outline of the carapace is nearly round. Mostly dull red, but the tips of its pinchers are black.

Oregon Rock Crab

Photo 5 p. 18

A strange-looking crab — a treat to find — is the Turtle Crab, *Cryptolithodes sitchensis*. The flat 4 to 7 cm carapace is so large compared to its body that none of the legs is visible from above; it is variously called the Turtle Crab, the Umbrella Crab, and the Butterfly Crab. The underside of the carapace is almost completely white, but the upper side varies considerably, being red, purple-red, gray, or brown, and sometimes streaked or blotched. Unfortunately the Turtle Crab is uncommon, but beachcombers occasionally find one under the rocks during extreme low tides, and divers occasionally bring one ashore where its strange shape causes excitement among shore enthusiasts.

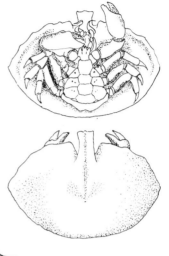

Turtle Crab

A bizarre crab looking something like an armored car: the Puget Sound King Crab, *Lopholithodes mandtii*. Though rarely seen intertidally, the juveniles are occasionally found under the rocks at extremely low tides. The young are brilliant orange or red with lavender or purple tinges; the adults less brilliant. The very thick and horny carapace grows to 30 cm in diameter. Pick one of these up: the crab folds its legs under its body for protection, goes into a rigid state, and becomes like a stony-hard box.

Puget Sound King Crab

Photo 4 p. 18

141

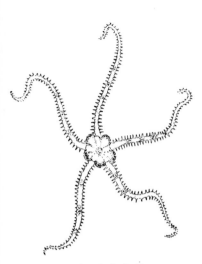

Daisy Brittle Star

Photo 46 p. 31

Under rocks and shell and on the holdfasts of kelp, brittle stars move about with writhing snake-like motions. The arms are fragile and break easily; handle brittle stars carefully. However, a brittle star pinned down under a shifting rock can break off an arm or two and get away; within a few weeks the arms grow back.

Though many species live offshore in deeper water, only one, the Daisy Brittle Star, *Ophiopholis aculeata*, is really abundant on rocky shores. A small body about 1 cm in diameter, with five long and very slender arms, up to 8 cm in length, and covered with warty prickly spines. The central disc is indented where the rays attach, forming flower-like lobes between. The Daisy Brittle Star is one of our most beautiful species; generally a white oral surface with variously colored central disc and rays: grays, browns, yellows, oranges, and reds.

The dainty Black and White Brittle Star, *Amphipholis pugetana*, occasionally slithers over the tops of exposed rocks at night. The small body generally .5 to 1 cm across and the legs eight to ten times the length of the body. This species is less likely than some to lose its rays. Though rare intertidally, it frequently occurs in immense numbers high in the subtidal zones, a condition which aids in its survival. It feeds on diatoms and particles of decaying plant and animal matter.

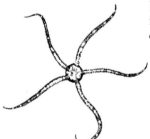

Black & White Brittle Star

On some rocky outcrops whole cities of mysterious round holes have been adopted by chitons, crabs, and sea anemones. The holes, about the size of walnuts, are probably the empty burrows of dead Piddock Clams, *Penitella penita*. This common rock boring clam, about 7 to 8 cm long, has a strange-looking shell divided into several distinct parts. Though the shell looks thin and fragile, the clam can burrow into sandstone, hard clay, basalt rock, and even concrete, by twisting and rocking on its foot which grips its support. Some biologists think that the clam uses chemicals, though no one has found an acid-forming gland. The burrow is a permanent home; only the long siphons project outward to bring in food and water. To look at a live Piddock Clam, break open one of its burrows, but use discretion: unthinking, over-ambitious diggers destroy the natural landscape of our beaches.

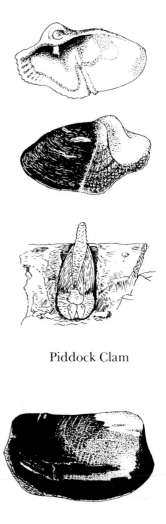

Piddock Clam

Another unusual clam commonly living among broken rocks and crevices and occasionally found attaching itself to floats by byssus threads, the Rock-dwelling Clam, *Entodesma saxicola*, is also called the Northwest Ugly Clam. Oblong and very irregular, it takes various shapes according to its habitat. A thick, dull olive-brown skin covers the surface of the 12 to 15 cm shell, and when the skin dries it shrinks, becomes brittle and cracks apart, often shattering the shell. The inside shell is glossy white and iridescent.

Rock-dwelling Clam

Before leaving the rocky shore, be sure to turn the rocks back over, fill in any holes, and put the animals back into their own habitats, or cover them with protective seaweeds. Leave the beach and the plants and animals that live there as you found them.

96 Beach grasses stabilize the sand dunes at Long Beach, Vancouver Island, B.C.

The Sandy Beach

Approach some sandy beaches through the battle line between the forest and the sand dunes, and then go on to the continuous line of wind-built dunes themselves. At the forest edge of the dunes the living mound of sand flows freely and unmercifully into mature hemlock and cedar. The whitened trunks of dead trees lean half buried and at angles to the sandy slope, like bristles along an old worn nail brush. Not a single plant or animal can survive long enough to gain a foothold. The bare sand of the twenty-meter-high dune glistens in the summer sun.

Going to the top of the leeward dune is hard work because the steep slope and falling sand make climbing difficult. But once on top! The view is spectacular: a continuous line of wind-swept ridges extending over a broad expanse to the sea; subdued grays, browns, lavenders, and purples painting a moody picture of life and death struggles in a beautiful but desolate land. A view most impressive during spring and summer when the seascape is brightened by the showy blooms of highly colored flowers.

But here on the ridge only a few hardy pioneer plants survive. These have root systems which reach into the deep sand for water and help keep the plants from being buried in the shifting sand. The wind continuously blows landward and the blown sand accumulates around the stems and root systems of plants and grasses which have managed to establish themselves, and builds up miniature mounds on the top of the dunes at the base of the plants. The most obvious plant, European Beach Grass, spreads its system of creeping underground stems and establishes a mat-like surface. Nearby are similarly built mounds of Yellow Abronia — striking clusters of bright yellow flowers surviving by very thick fleshy tap-roots that penetrate a meter or more into the sand. Another mound builder is Silver Beach-weed, a silvery plant covered with silky hairs and also having a thick fleshy tap-root. But this plant, like the others, erodes away as the sand moves along the ridge.

Above Beach

The descent to the shore is down a very gradual slope. Scattered over its surface lie masses of Beach Morning Glory, the shiny leaves and trailing vines gracing the otherwise barren sand with clusters of trumpet-shaped pink and white flowers.

On the low-lying area the landscape changes: the sand underneath is moist, being nearer the water table, and together with a stable bottom creates a more favorable place for plants and grasses to establish and survive. This area is a scented gallery of grasses and herbs and shrubs of all sizes and shapes. A silky shrub with short leafy branches, the Bush Lupine with its yellow or pale blue or pink brush of flowers. A larger shrub, Scotch Broom, a fast spreading species with yellow pea-shaped flowers. Among the shrubs, and occasionally forming miniature forests, small stands of sturdy Beach Pines. Throughout the pines, the low growing Beach Strawberries, Evening Primroses, and Beach Peas painting the seascape with their showy pink, purple, and lavender blooms. In the open spaces, tall, solitary, white beach flowers: the white, flat-topped clusters of Yarrow; the white, papery heads of Pearly Everlasting. Everywhere, wheat-colored, sweet-scented grasses, Beach Grass, Large Headed Sedge and Salt Rush. These are the last brave plants to creep out over the barren sandy plain separating the dunes from the sea.

Between the offshore waters and the upper part of the beach lies the shoreline, a long white crescent laced with bubbling arches of foam. An invasion of waves rolls gently against the sloping bottom, loses momentum, and breaks into surf before reaching shore, each final movement forming intricate ripple marks in the soft wet sand. This sandy beach sets a timeless and unhurried rhythm: grain by grain the sand leisurely comes and goes along the shore, now building, now receding, with the constant motion of the winds and waves.

As the tide goes out, the broad expanse of beach appears to be barren and fit only for building sandcastles, but shorebirds feeding along the tide line confirm that the shore is swarming with life. The animals are not visible on the surface: they are buried underground. Clams and worms dominate.

Sandy beaches on the surf-swept outer coast are impossible as habitats for most seashore creatures. The clean coarse sand is constantly stirred by strong wave action and by the rise and fall of the tides. Thus, the only large animals able to survive the surf burrow under the sand or move up and down the beach with the tides. Typically, several species of shrimp swim in shallow water and follow the tide; hordes of Large Beach Hoppers burrow under the sand in the Spray Zone and move down the slope with the tide; and stream-lined Razor Clams burrow rapidly in the surf at the low tide line.

Sandy beaches in protected areas frequently become mixed with fine mud, and have a richer assortment of microscopic animals and a greater variety and number of larger inhabitants than exposed sandy beaches. Cockles, Sand Clams, and Tellens move slowly through the sand, most living deep below the surface and the adults barely able to move. Tube-dwelling worms glue sand grains together to form homes so fragile that they would be destroyed on the surf-swept outer coast. On some protected beaches eelgrass beds stabilize the bottom and prevent the sand from being carried away, the massive root structures and tangled blades providing shelter for a variety of amphipods, isopods, snails, nudibranchs, crabs, and fish.

Though burrowing animals are relatively safe from wave action and from drying out, their huge numbers attract a variety of opportunist predators. When the tide goes out, gulls and sandpipers and sanderlings probe and dig along the shore, but when the beach is submerged it becomes a hunting ground for flatfish which move in from deep water to gobble up small clams, snails, and crustaceans. Hungry sea stars, notably the Pink Star, the Sun Star, the Purple Star, and the Sunflower Star, range widely and creep onto sandy beaches to prey on clams at the surface. Many predatory burrowers follow the clams below the surface into their own world, including predatory sea snails such as the giant-sized Moon Snail and a variety of carnivorous worms which eat any animal they can manage, dead or alive.

Among the beach grasses above high tide line the lacy tracks of the graceful Snowy Plovers, *Charadrius alexandrinus*, run everywhere. These birds sprint along swiftly and silently, blending so perfectly with the sand that they become the little "ghosts" of the sand dunes. The backs of the plump sparrow-sized Snowy Plovers are the color of dry sand; the underparts are white; a black chest band reduces to a crescent at each side of the breast. They feed on insects and flies, occasionally tripping down to the shore to scavenge in the decaying debris at the tide line. Snowy Plovers breed along the open beaches and dunes, frequently in Oregon and southern Washington but rarely in British Columbia. They seldom make a nest, but lay their two to three olive-buff eggs in a hollow high above the beach and leave them for the wind to cover with drifting sand. In winter many Snowy Plovers migrate south; only a few are resident.

Snowy Plover

Along the tidal mud flats and sand bars, whistling mournful calls and making quick forward movements and brief stops, run the Black-bellied Plovers, *Pluvialis squatarola*. These fairly large and wild and wary travellers are among the most striking of our shorebirds. In summer the head and neck and mantle are a mottled white and gray; a broad white mark carries from the bill, over the eye, and down to the shoulders; the face, bill, and breast are jet black; below-tail and under-wings, always white. In fall and winter the black fades to the dry gray of the sand, blending so well with the dune sand that as long as they remain motionless the birds frequently go unnoticed. The Black-bellied Plovers winter along our coast, but in April or May migrate to their breeding grounds in Alaska, both sexes wearing identical black-breasted "suits".

Black-bellied Plover
summer and winter plumage

A group of delightful sandpipers, no larger than sparrows, run along the tide line in stops and starts. Popularly called "peeps": when alarmed they take flight in great flocks, filling the air with a chorus of soft peepings. They perform amazing antics in unison, as if performing to a prearranged signal; one instant they show a cloud of black backs, but on the next display their white under-parts; then, after a few turns, settle down again to the same spot and resume their feeding.

Western Sandpiper

The largest and most abundant of the "peeps" is the Western Sandpiper, *Calidris mauri*, slightly larger than 15 cm. This species has a long black bill that tips slightly downward, a rusty-red head and shoulders, a pale breast, and black legs. It breeds in northwestern Alaska and migrates up and down the Pacific coast, feeding along the way on insects and tiny crustaceans at the low tide line. The smal-lest, called the Least Sandpiper, *Calidris minutilla* (not pictured) is streaked dark brown above and on the breast, but white below. Identify them by their legs: they are greenish-yellow, not black, and the toes are not webbed like those of other peeps. Though commonly found scavenging alongside the Western Sandpipers at the low tide line, Least Sandpipers prefer areas farther back in the dry mud and sand.

Sanderling
winter plumage

Perky bands of little peeps keep company with the sandpipers — the delightful Sanderlings, *Calidris alba*. In winter Sanderlings are one of the palest shorebirds, being mottled gray above, with darker shoulders and wings, and white below, blending beautifully with the sand; but during the spring breeding season, the adults sport a rich rusty color over much of the body. Sanderlings lack a hind toe and show black flashing wing stripes during flight. They are common spring and fall migrants along our tidal sand flats, stopping briefly on their way to the Arctic tundra to nest. In August or September they pass back along the shoreline on their way to wintering grounds in the Southern Hemisphere. A few are year-round residents.

When walking above the high tide line, explore the old logs and planks stranded by the falling tide or tossed up on the shore by storm waves. Many are riddled with countless holes or burrows; if the holes go very deep and are the size of a pencil, they are the work of one of the several species of Shipworms, *Bankia setacea*. The burrows follow the grain of the wood and do not cut into or cross one another; nor do they move from board to board. Split the wood open to find the live animal inside, or the empty burrow in which the animal has died and disintegrated. Though Shipworms live in the wooden hulls of ships and dock pilings, the name is misleading because the animal is not a worm, but really a clam with two tiny shells near the front end, and with its long slender worm-like body encased in a tube manufactured by the animal. When young it is a free-swimming larva, but after a few weeks it attaches itself to a piece of wood and immediately begins to bore a hole by closing and opening its shells, and by rocking back and forth. It cements its end permanently to the opening and puts out its siphon tips through which to feed. During its lifetime, as the Shipworm grows, it digs a winding route through the plank; then, having no more space, it dies.

Shipworm

Gribble

While Shipworms work deep inside of wood, Gribbles, *Limnoria lignorum*, work very close to the surface. They are isopods about 3 mm long and seldom burrow deeper than 2 or 3 cm, possibly because of a difficulty in breathing. They work quickly and can completely bury themselves in the wood in from four to six days. They rasp away with the mouth and as fast as they gouge it out they pass the small particles through the digestive tract. This animal takes all its nourishment from the wood. Gribbles and Shipworms cause so much damage to wood floats, docks, dock piling, and wooden ships that they are known as the "termites of the sea".

The same logs riddled with shipworms may be colonized on the outside by Pelagic Goose Barnacles, *Lepas anatifera*, a large-stalked barnacle up to 20 cm with five plates covering the body. The finely striated plates are dirty white or bluish-gray, with bright orange edges; the stalk, purplish-brown. This barnacle forms massive colonies by attaching itself to hard surfaces, such as floating logs, old bottles, and stalks of kelp, and creates a floating island which travels great distances, and which may become stranded on the beach during storms and high tides.

Pelagic Goose Barnacle

Sea Nettle

Photo 78 p. 43

Moon Jellyfish

Photo 77 p. 43

When strolling on the beach, especially in the spring, summer, and fall, watch for any of several species of bell-shaped jellyfish that become stranded during storms and high tides. A very impressive one found on our beaches, the Sea Nettle, *Cyanea capillata*, is a huge blob of perhaps 60 cm across and large enough to fill a small washtub. The huge transparent mass may be milk-colored or tinted an orange, yellow, or brown. Eight clusters of tentacles extend from the bell and each cluster has a hundred tentacles which may trail two meters in length: the common name is Lion's Mane. The tentacles have stinging cells which are normally used to capture planktonic prey, and small crustaceans and fish. The Sea Nettle is the only common jellyfish in our area which can cause a severe and nasty rash in humans. Avoid it! Do not touch it even when it is washed up on the beach and is dead.

A softly shining jellyfish with a fringe of short tentacles hanging down from the halfmoon-shaped bell, the Moon Jellyfish, *Aurelia aurita*, occasionally moves into quiet bays and estuaries in immense numbers. When stranded on the beach it is a flattened colorless blob, except for the pink, brown, or yellow horseshoe-shaped reproductive organs. The Moon Jellyfish is smaller than the Sea Nettle, usually 10 to 15 cm in length, and capable of stinging, but for most humans the sting is never severe.

The Water Jellyfish, *Aequorea aequorea*, travels in huge swarms during the summer. This one is actually a free-swimming stage in the life cycle of one of the hydroids. It has a clear thick gelatinous bell from 7 to 10 cm in diameter and over fifty tentacles capable of great extension used in gathering food. The Water Jellyfish is highly luminescent when disturbed; at night it often looks like a shimmering ball of light. Like the Moon Jellyfish, this species is harmless to most people.

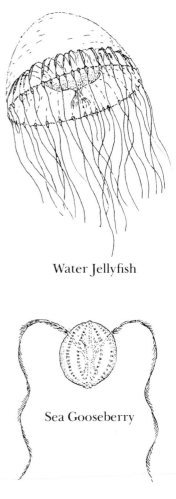

Water Jellyfish

All along the beach, little oval balls of clear jelly the size of marbles, the Sea Gooseberries, *Pleurobrachia bachei*, pop underfoot. The same shape and texture as jellyfish, but unlike jellyfish, which propel themselves by pulsating movement, Sea Gooseberries propel themselves by large paddle-like hairs or "combs", and therefore belong to a group of animals called "comb jellies". Sea Gooseberries are about 1.5 cm long with two tentacles of 15 cm when extended. Really quite harmless. Pick some up and put them into a jar of sea water to watch them move.

Sea Gooseberry

Where the long hours of direct sunlight have dried out the upper surface of loose sand, notice the mysterious little holes and domes. High on the beach beyond the highest reaches of high tides and storm waves, insects run down from the dunes to burrow into sand or hide under beach debris, many of them, particularly the beetles, preying on other insects.

Dig just above the high water line where there are clusters of nearly rounded holes in nearly moist sand, or sort through seaweed drifts, or turn over driftwood, for the delightful beach hoppers, or "sand fleas". During the heat of the day beach hoppers keep moist by burrowing into seaweed or sand, but at dusk they emerge from their burrows to move closer to the edge of the water. At night, visit the beach with a flashlights to see whole herds of frisky beach hoppers jumping about and scavenging for food in decaying seaweeds. At dawn they orient themselves by the moon and find their way back to their burrows on the upper part of the beach.

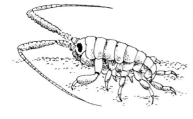

California
Beach Hopper

The largest beach hopper in our region, but found only on exposed beaches, is the California Beach Hopper, *Orchestoidea californiana*, which reaches a body length of about 2.5 cm, and has a pair of long bright orange antennae that more than doubles the length. Generally the body is grayish, ivory-white, or brownish-white.

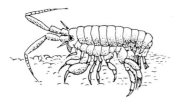

Small Beach Hopper

A smaller but more abundant version and one mainly on protected beaches is the Small Beach Hopper, *Orchestia traskiana*. Easy to distinguish because of its smaller size, about 2 cm, its darker grayish color, and its antennae which are not brightly colored.

When high tides lap at the shore, walk along the high water line to discover a variety of small crustaceans, amphipods, isopods, and small shrimp which follow the waves or live just under the surface of the sand. If a wave dislodges them, they lose no time in burying themselves back into sand. Drag a fine-meshed net through shallow water near the high tide line, and put the catch in a jar filled with sea water.

Water-line Isopod

A tiny active isopod that follows the tides, the little Water-line Isopod, *Cirolana kincaidi*, has a voracious appetite and helps other scavengers of the sandy beach clean up dead and decaying plants and animals. Observe a dead fish or bird for two or three days: a horde of Water-line Isopods will swarm over it and reduce it to a bare white skeleton.

A small shrimp abundant in shallow waters, the Opossum Shrimp, or Mysid, *Archaeomysis grebnitzkii*, grows 4 to 8 cm in length, and like the possum the female carries the young in a brood pouch under her thorax. The grayish, nearly transparent body blends with the sandy and muddy bottom, but provides a clear view of the internal action as the shrimp eats, swims, and breathes. Even a view of the eggs in the female's brood pouch is provided during the spring and summer months.

Opossum Shrimp

Another small shrimp that swims in shallow water where the waves lap the shore is the Crago Shrimp, *Crago* sp., most growing to a length of 5 or 6 cm. Like the other crustaceans following the tides, they are well camouflaged, a sandy mottled combination of gray, brown, and black. The long delicate antennae serve as sense organs to detect food and warn of approaching danger.

Crago Shrimp

An unusual amphipod disappears back under the sand the instant water sloshes over it, the Hairy Amphipod, *Eohaustorius washingtonianus*, only 5 to 8 mm in length. The legs are fringed with numerous long hairs: therefore its hairy appearance. This amphipod is restricted to sandy beaches where it feeds on decaying plant and animal matter and on diatoms that settle to the bottom.

Hairy Amphipod

155

On a relatively protected beach where the sand is mixed with mud, the giant Moon Snail, *Polinices lewisii*, plows its way along at the surface or buries itself completely in the sand. Its light brown shell is one of the largest on our coast, about 12 cm in height, made up almost entirely of one great whorl with about five smaller whorls forming a distinct spiral. Stop a while to watch. When the Moon Snail travels through the sand, its enormous fleshy foot almost wraps around its shell, but should the snail pull itself inside it squeezes out a considerable amount of water through perforations located around the edge of that fleshy foot. The Moon Snail is not often seen for it finds its food by burrowing below the surface and drilling a hole through the shells of clams, snails, mussels, and oysters with its radula, or occasionally by suffocating its victim with that enormous foot. On protected sandy beaches and on mud flats in the spring and summer, Moon Snails lay thousands of tiny eggs which become pressed together with particles of sand to form a collar-like ring about the snail's shell. The sand is cemented together by a sticky mucous which then hardens and forms rubberized "sand collars". During high tide at about mid-summer, the egg case crumbles and a half million or so free-swimming larvae — potential Moon Snails — are released into the sea. Do not pick up the collars and throw them around: they break or dry out and thousands of Moon Snail eggs die.

Moon Snail
Photo 23 p. 23

On the open coast where beating surf creates clean sandy beaches, the dainty little Purple Olive Snail, *Olivella biplicata*, grows to about 2 cm in length. The Purple Olive is easy to recognize: it is one of the few species on our coast to have a smooth and polished shell, grayish-brown with dark purplish lines outlining the edges of the whorls. The olive-shaped central body whorl is comparatively long and narrow, allowing for the animal's very large foot which curves back over the snail, nearly covering it as the animal pushes through sand. The Purple Olive is a scavenger feeding on decaying plant and animal matter. The shells have always been a favorite among shell collectors, but the pretty shells are rare: collect only empty ones.

Another animal partly or completely buried in muddy sand with the Moon Snail — the familiar Sand Dollar, *Dendraster excentricus*, measures up to 8 cm in diameter. Sand Dollars are closely related to sea urchins and sea stars, but have flattened bodies and tube feet and spines so small and densely packed that the living animal looks and feels like velvet. As the Sand Dollar plows slowly along, it selects grains of sand covered with edible particles, such as diatoms and detritus, and passes them along food tracts located on the underside and lined with microscopic hairs. Sand Dollars often lie half buried in the sand with the upper surface slanting in the direction of the current. Because they avoid heavy surf and prefer the protection of deeper water offshore, living specimens are seen less frequently than the familiar white tests, or shells, cast up on the beach during high tides. Living specimens range in color from grays to charcoal-reds and deep purple.

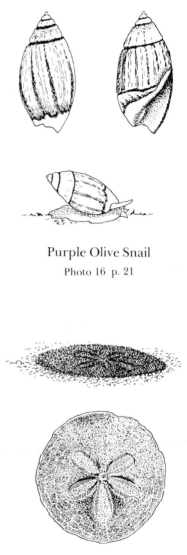

Purple Olive Snail
Photo 16 p. 21

Sand Dollar

Eelgrass

Photo 91 p. 47

On protected beaches, where the bottom is a mixture of sand and mud, plants called Eelgrass, *Zostera marina*, grow. Their long, thin, bright green grass-like blades are 5 to 10 mm wide and a meter or more in length. The thick tangled roots stabilize the beach and prevent winds and currents from carrying away the sand. The stable bottom and massive eelgrass beds provide protected homes for many kinds of animals, some of which depend on one another for survival. In addition the beds are rich in food supplies: diatoms, bacteria, decaying plant and animal matter, and the eelgrass leaves themselves provide food for a variety of species. Visit an eelgrass bed during the spring and summer when the beds achieve their greatest growth and support the largest variety of plants and animals. Take time to sort through the fronds and stems to see various species of algae, amphipods, isopods, snails, nudibranchs, shrimps, crabs, bryozoans, and fish which sit on the leaves, dart over the surface, or settle among the roots and burrow under the sand.

An alga sure to be growing on the leaves of eelgrass, especially during the spring and summer, Red Fringe, *Smithora naiadum*, is very noticeable because of its bright purplish-red color and its very thin broad blades — 2 to 10 cm long — joined onto the eelgrass by minute narrow stalks. Red Fringe also grows on surfgrass and on kelps on rocky shores.

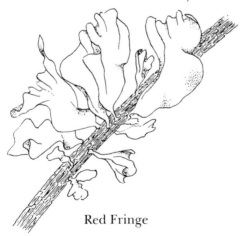

Red Fringe

An odd-looking animal clings tightly to the leaves of eelgrass, the Skeleton Shrimp, *Caprella* sp., not really a shrimp, but an amphipod with a long skinny body. In eelgrass a Skeleton Shrimp is well camouflaged, for its green color and long body — about 4 cm — make it difficult to spot. When feeding it clings to the leaves by its three hind pairs of claws and patiently waits for small organisms and other morsels to drift by; then, with lightning speed, it snaps them up with a pair of claws located near the head.

Pull the leaves of eelgrass tightly between your fingers to locate and dislodge the transparent green Eelgrass Isopod, *Idotea resecata*. Because of its color and the seven pairs of legs it uses to cling tightly and flatly to the leaves, the Eelgrass Isopod is difficult to find. This creature is the counterpart of the Rockweed Isopod that scurries along the rocky shore: both species are the same size, about 4 cm, but the Eelgrass Isopod is green and the tip of its tail curves inward instead of outward.

Skeleton Shrimp
Photo 11 p. 20

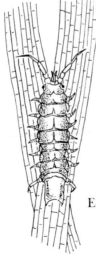

Eelgrass Isopod

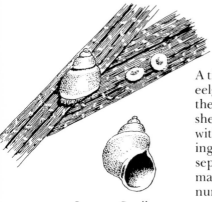

Lacuna Snail

A tiny plump snail moves with a distinct waddle on eelgrass and on the blades and holdfasts of kelp, the Lacuna Snail, *Lacuna variegata*. Its very tiny shell, about 5 mm in height, is usually light brown with lighter bands, the first whorl above the opening taking up most of the shell and a deep slit separating the first and second whorl. Its egg masses look like miniature yellow life-savers, great numbers of individual eggs enclosed in each ring.

In places where eelgrass grows on mud or sand, a small rounded slug-like snail dwells, the Bubble Snail, *Haminoea virescens*, an unusual-looking snail with the sides of its foot modified into wing-like flaps for swimming. The thin fragile shell consists of one large body whorl, and only partially protects the snail because its proportionately larger body and foot can scarcely be pulled in: the shell reaches about 1 cm in length, but the snail, when fully extended, may reach a length of 2 or 3 cm. The over-all color is dull green or dull yellow with some scattered lighter flecks. In the spring and summer the egg capsules look like tiny colorless balloons on eelgrass leaves or on the sand.

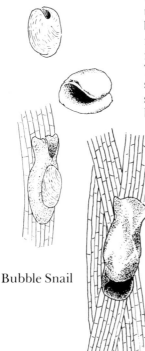

Bubble Snail

A very pretty and well camouflaged sea slug that lives only on the larger leaves of eelgrass, the Green Sea Slug, *Phyllaplysia taylori*, is transparent green with longitudinal black and yellow stripes. Mature specimens are about 4 cm in length and are just a little wider than the width of the widest leaves of eelgrass. The Green Sea Slug is not a nudibranch, but is closely related to the land slug.

A curious animal looking like something out of a carnival, the Hooded Nudibranch, *Melibe leonina*, has its head expanded into a broad hood fringed with numerous slender tentacles and along its back six flattened gill-like structures, cerata, looking like broad leaves. The animal feeds by using its hood and tentacles to rake in small organisms floating in the water, especially amphipods. It swims by making thrashing movements and can drift for long periods at the surface by trapping air in its hood. Large for a nudibranch, almost 10 cm, and grayish or almost colorless. Look for the Hooded Nudibranch in eelgrass and in kelp beds.

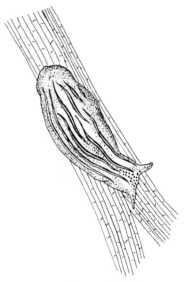

Green Sea Slug
Photo 36 p. 26

Another nudibranch that looks something like a shaggy mouse is aptly named the Shaggy Mouse Nudibranch, *Aeolidea papillosa*, 6 to 7 cm. Whitish or pinkish with some gray or brown spots, the numerous cerata grayish-brown or almost colorless, the Shaggy Mouse is a close relative of the Opalescent Nudibranch — both commonly found on protected rocky shores and in eelgrass beds on protected sandy beaches.

Hooded Nudibranch
Photo 40 p. 27

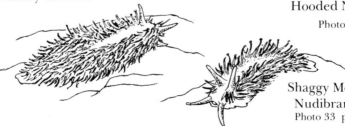

Shaggy Mouse
Nudibranch
Photo 33 p. 26

An odd jellyfish attaches itself to eelgrass and sometimes to kelp, the Stalked Jellyfish, *Haliclystus auricula*. Quite different in appearance from most of its relatives, it has a stalk which grows to 2.5 cm in height and has eight clusters of tentacles, each tipped with nearly a hundred stinging cells borne on a short knob. The iridescent green, yellow, orange, and brown Stalked Jellyfish feeds almost exclusively on the Skeleton Shrimp so numerous on eelgrass leaves. The Stalked Jellyfish moves very slowly by using its pads and the adhesive basal stalk by which it attaches to the eelgrass, but if dislodged this one is unable to swim like normal jellyfish and may fall to the sand and die.

Stalked Jellyfish

Photo 79 p. 43

During the summer large numbers of brilliantly colored Orange Jellyfish, *Gonionemus vertens*, attach to eelgrass and kelp with sticky pads located near the tips of their long tentacles. When dislodged, these swim like other jellyfish until they manage to attach again. The tiny Orange Jellyfish has a height of only 1.5 cm, and a width slightly larger than the height; the bell is yellow-green; the four ribbon-like reproductive organs, deep orange-red; and sixty to seventy short tentacles hang in a transparent fringe from the edge of the bell. They feed on small crustaceans, such as amphipods and the larvae of fishes.

Orange Jellyfish

At low tide, where protective eelgrass beds or depressions in the sand hold a little water, a variety of small fish lie half buried in the sand, and in shallow water dart off in all directions. One of the most abundant species lies on one side and looks in two directions at once: the Sand Sole, *Psettichthys melanosticus*, about 20 cm in length. The mature Sand Sole is peculiar looking, a thin flat fish with both eyes on the uppermost side. These Sand Soles darting around on the eelgrass might be in different stages of maturity, many with one eye still migrating around the flattened body.

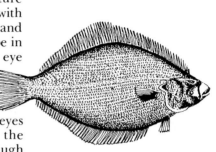

Sand Sole

Photo 81 p. 44

Another interesting fish buries itself up to its eyes on protected sandy or muddy beaches, the Staghorn Sculpin, *Leptocottus armatus*. Though similar to the Tidepool Sculpin found on rocky shores, this more streamlined version is larger, some specimens reaching a length of 25 to 30 cm. Generally gray or olive-green above, the underside off-white with a faint yellow tinge. A black blotch on the dorsal fin distinguishes this one from other sculpins, and this species inhabits areas where incoming fresh water reduces salinity.

Staghorn Sculpin

The bright green Penpoint Gunnel, *Apodichthys flavidus*, takes its name from the peculiar anal fin that resembles the old-fashioned penpoints that had to be dipped in ink bottles. Typically the same color as eelgrass, though various shades of yellow, brown, and red do occur. This common blenny has a dark line running downward from the eyes and often has a dark line or light spots running along the sides. It reaches a length of 45 cm.

Penpoint Gunnel

Photo 82 p. 45

163

In the protected shallow pools, and especially in eelgrass beds, a large crab marches briskly along or hides beneath the surface of sand — only a pair of antennae, a mouth, and eyes protruding — the Dungeness Crab, *Cancer magister*, the familiar species in commercial markets. It generally occurs in deep water and ranges widely, sometimes travelling a mile a day, but often coming into shallow bays to molt, especially in early summer. The Dungeness Crab has a larger body than the similar Red Rock Crab, up to 20 cm across the carapace: the claws, however, are proportionately smaller, the shell not nearly so thick, and the color light brownish-orange instead of deep reddish-purple. To find one, use a long forked stick to probe the eelgrass beds for a large heavy lump under the sand. The male has a narrow V-shaped abdominal "flap" on the underside; the female has a wide U-shaped "flap".

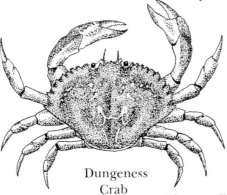

Dungeness
Crab

Photo 6 p. 18

That small spider crab basking at the surface of eelgrass is a Graceful Kelp Crab, *Pugettia gracilis*. The top side of the carapace, 2 to 3 cm wide, has a number of short spines on which the crab drapes pieces of eelgrass and other debris for camouflage. Unlike the more sluggish spider crabs which encourage the growth of sponges or bryozoans on their backs, the Graceful Kelp Crab prefers to keep its carapace clean. Generally dark reddish-brown.

Graceful Kelp Crab

Dig deep into clean sand on protected beaches and
quiet bays in the same general area as the Moon
Snails and Sand Dollars to find the Sand Clam,
Macoma secta, a species with long separate siphons
which allow it to live well below the surface, 30 to
40 cm deep. The Sand Clam closely resembles its
mud flat relative, the Bent-nosed Clam, but the
thin white shells of the Sand Clam are larger,
about 10 cm, and wedge-shaped, lacking the
"bent-nose" twist in the shell. When completely
open the empty shells lying at the surface look like
wings; hence the name Butterfly Clam . The
Sand Clam makes very good eating, but is found
only in small numbers.

Sand Clam

Another sand-loving clam lives in scattered pockets along the coast, the dainty Tellen Clam, *Tel-
lina bodegensis*, with its glossy white fragile shell
slightly bent, pointed to the front, and rounded to
the rear. The size varies considerably, but the average height is about 3 cm. The Tellen Clam has a
shell with numerous distinct concentric lines on
the shell.

Tellen Clam

At the lowest tide levels on the violent surf-swept beaches of the outer coast burrows the notoriously fast Razor Clam, *Siliqua patula*. Its thin and brittle shells are polished tan or olive-green, about 15 cm long and shaped like an old-fashioned straight razor. Razor Clams stay near the surface of the sand when feeding, but to survive in that violent world they speedily dig downward through the sand 2 or 3 cm every second. When digging, the muscular foot points downward, extending to a length of half the shell; the tip of the foot expands to form an anchor; the muscle contracts and pulls the clam downward rapidly, again, and again, and again. Razor Clams have fragile shells in spite of their wild habitat. Dig for only the larger specimens and keep every damaged one you find because they soon die if damaged and returned to the beach — and follow the legal limits on the size and numbers.

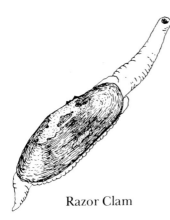

Razor Clam

Those small holes at the surface of mud or sand are often the work of Proboscis Worms, *Glycera rugosa*, large and active, light yellowish in color, and composed of two hundred or more segments: thus the name Corrugated Worm. This fierce species can convert its long pointed head into a club-shaped structure by extending the proboscis which is armed with four, hook-like black jaws. When capturing prey and when digging rapidly into sand the worm extends and withdraws the proboscis rapidly and regularly, like a battering ram. A number of related worms with long segmented bodies and extendible mouth parts can be expected in muddy, sandy, or cobblestone habitats, and in amongst barnacles, mussels, and in seaweed holdfasts. All are capable of biting the hand which holds them!

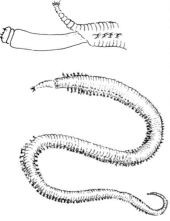

Proboscis Worm

In quiet bays, under pieces of wood and debris at the surface, or in shallow burrows in any combination of mud, sand, or gravel, lives the impressive Sand Worm, *Nereis vexillosa*. Large and fleshy; varying in length from 5 to 30 cm; tan with a beautiful green, blue, or pink iridescence. The Sand Worm is most impressive when it expands its paddle-like feet for swimming or when it extends its heavy jaws for feeding on algae and on small animals, or even on other worms. Handle this wiggly worm with care: the heavy jaws can break skin.

Sand Worm

On exposed sandy beaches at about the mid-tide zone, or lower, a smooth flattened worm, the Sand Nemertean, *Cerebratulus* sp., may be 1 cm wide and reach a length of 30 cm or more. This worm has conspicuous slits on either side of the head and a little "tail". Adults tend to be brown or red; the young usually gray or pink. The Sand Nemertean is extremely fragile, the body breaking into pieces when handled, and the little tail falling off, but all nemerteans have great powers of regeneration and pieces larger than 1 cm can grow into whole new nemerteans. The Sand Nemertean has a huge, specialized proboscis that extends to wrap around a prey, such as another worm, and swallows it whole. Once filled, this species can survive without food for long periods, up to a year.

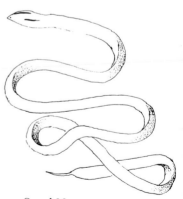

Sand Nemertean

Dig down into the sand just below the mid-tide level on a protected beach to find a strange-looking sea cucumber often mistaken for a worm, the Burrowing Sea Cucumber, *Leptosynapta clarki.* This animal lacks the tube feet common to most other cucumbers, and instead has a slippery skin armed with numerous microscopic hooks that stiffen the body and anchor it to the bottom. The mouth is surrounded by twelve tentacles which are much smaller than those of other sea cucumbers. As the animal travels along swallowing sand the tentacles sift detritus and diatoms and other microscopic foods that cling to sand grains. Dirty white with a pink or orange tinge, the Burrowing Sea Cucumber has a diameter of 1.5 to 2.5 cm, and may be 5 to 6 cm when extended. Pick up this cucumber and it will cling to your fingers by its anchor-like hooks, but don't be surprised if some come off on your hands.

Burrowing
Sea Cucumber

During extreme low tides a feather-like plume may be visible in shallow water, the Sea Pen, *Ptilosarcus gurneyi,* seldom found intertidally but frequent in large beds in deeper water offshore. When submerged and fully expanded it resembles an old-fashioned pen made from an ostrich plume. Beautifully colored, from pale pinks to bright oranges. Like sea anemones, Sea Pens are carnivorous and capture their small prey with the numerous little tentacles located on the plume-like branches. When stroked or moved by currents in the dark, they give off a greenish luminescent light. Sea Pens are capable of retracting into the sediment when disturbed, and any attempt to dislodge one might destroy the animal because it has a bulbous foot which acts as an anchor on the bottom.

Sea Pen

Photo 76 p. 42

Before leaving the sandy beach be sure to fill in any holes: small clams may be washed out, or killed by predators; or the piles of sand may kill many clams or other animals whose burrows cannot reach the surface.

97 Ripple marks decorate tidal flats at Willapa Bay, Wa.

The Mud Flat

Go along a dirt path that follows a small slow-moving fresh-water stream lined with Alder, Vine Maple, and Coast Willow. Along the stream, on both sides, Cattails, Bull Rushes, and Bull Thistle. In places thorny tangled Blackberries nearly covering the surface of the stream. The sweet-smelling grasses, Giant Vetch, Salt Rush, and Arrow Grass, crowding the banks. Pickleweed and Saltwort, those odd plants with jointed leafless stems, spreading moss-green mats in shallow pools and tidal channels, and covered only by the highest tides. These last plants creep into the chocolate-colored ripple marks separating the edge of the shoreline from the broad expanse of mud flat.

Mud flats occur where a river or a stream enters a bay or inland channel and deposits muddy sand, and because mud mixes with sand or gravel any combination is possible. Some are very firm and hard-packed, while others are like soup. But mud flats exist only on the most protected shores because strong currents or wave action would carry the mud and sandy sediments out to sea. All true mud flats are, however, subject to the rise and fall of the tides.

As the tide goes out, the mud flat looks disappointing: plants and animals are not nearly so obvious or so spectacular as that colorful collection on a rocky shore. Mud flat animals, though, are just as intriguing and may be just as abundant, but are, simply, living underground and out of sight — at least while the tide is out.

Mud flats support large populations of highly specialized animals, including many clams and snails, a few crustaceans, and whole armies of worms. Evidence? The little piles of sand or mud around the openings to burrows, coiled fecal castings of worms, countless rambling slime trails, and empty clam shells. The surface teems with many kinds of microscopic organisms, including diatoms, tiny amphipods, and isopods. Mud flats also often produce thick planktonic blooms which provide food for countless filter feeders.

For most rocky shore and sandy beach organisms, life in a mud flat would be extremely difficult because of the few hard surfaces to serve as places of attachment, and the great problems involved in breathing, moving, and food gathering. There are no sea urchins and few sea stars here, though sea stars do move down from rocky outcrops to prey upon clams and oysters. There are few animals here that breathe through the surface of their skins, and many fish and crabs cannot survive here because mud clogs their gills. On the other hand, animals that burrow under the surface are safe: wave action does not bother them, the blanket of mud protects them from extremes of temperature, and they are in little danger of becoming dry when the tide goes out. Basically, animals living on a mud flat live on only two habitats, either on the surface or in shallow burrows beneath it. Though zones do occur, they are difficult to observe because so many of the animals live below the sediments.

Whimbrel

On the drier upper regions of the mud flat a rather large bird picks and probes at the surface for insects, and occasionally thrusts its long down-curved bill deep into the mud, the Whimbrel, *Numenius phaeopus*. A second Whimbrel stands nearby, stork-like on one leg, now and then giving loud high pitched calls, "whee, whee", or rapid whistles, "ti, ti, ti", the vibrant voice sounding across the mud flat. Mottled grayish-brown upper parts, brown-streaked whitish underparts, dark striped crown, long darkish legs, and long down-curved bill. Whimbrels are regular migrants flying high in V's along our coast: they appear in April and May moving swiftly northward to their breeding grounds in Alaska, the Northwest Territories, and the Yukon, and appear again going south during August, September, and October.

Dunlin

Great numbers of tiny gray shorebirds, the Dunlins, *Calidris alpina*, gather by the hundreds and thousands into such great flocks that from a distance they appear to be long clouds of smoke. They twist and turn, as though disciplined to act as one bird, and then alight on the expansive reaches of the mud flat. At first they dash vigorously here and there searching for crustaceans and insects, but when their gullets are full the flock settles down to rest, most standing on one leg. Dunlins are the most common of our wintering shorebirds, often keeping company with the "peeps" on sand bars and mud flats or moving into wet farm fields. In winter Dunlins are grayish above and below and have no distinctive marks, but in summer they have a reddish mantle, streaked head, and a black patch on the underside. Dunlins are larger than peeps, and their darker back and blackish, down-curved and heavy bill distinguishes them from Sanderlings.

Above the high tide line a dozen or so distinctly marked shorebirds alternately run and then pause to look around, the familiar Killdeer, *Charadrius vociferus*. Well named "vociferous", they are among the noisiest of the noisy, literally shouting their name, "kill-dee, kill-dee", or nervously "hic-cuping", or fussily chattering loudly with their repertoire of other notes. These robin-sized birds nest in open places on the ground and deposit their spotted buff-colored eggs in shallow depressions lined with pebbles and broken shells. Tricksters, they decoy intruders from the breeding grounds: at the first cry of alarm the parent scurries away from the nest, faking injury, crying piteously, and holding one wing up while beating the ground wildly with the other. But having successfully lured away the intruding animal or human, the bird suddenly becomes well, springs up, and scolds severely. It may return to its nest to resume its duties, but occasionally follows the unhappy intruder for long distances, continuing its performance and disturbing the whole community. Killdeers are easy to identify by their behavior and by their distinct way of dressing: two striking black bands on a snowy neck and breast, brown above and pure white below, flesh-colored legs, black bill, and in flight showing reddish-yellow tail, and below-tail. Killdeers are year-round resident birds frequenting open mud flats, marshes, river banks, pastures, and dirt or gravel roads. They consume great quantities of insects, mostly grasshoppers, mosquitoes, beetles, flies, and insect larvae.

Killdeer

Running behind receding waves on exposed sandy beaches, or probing in protected mud flats, the Semipalmated Plovers, *Charadrius semipalmatus*, hunt for shellfish, crustaceans, worms, and insects. Like miniature killdeers, but with one instead of two black breast-bands and without the reddish-yellow tail and below-tail. Winter birds are similar, but with washed out colors, especially the black about the head. The toes are partly webbed or "simipalmated". Most of these little birds are known on our coastline as migrants only, passing to and from central California and their breeding grounds in Alaska and the Northwest Territories.

Semipalmated Plover
summer plumage

Standing motionless and statue-like in shallow water, with head folded into shoulders like an old man, the Great Blue Heron, *Ardea herodias*, patiently awaits its prey. Slowly, very slowly, he lifts each leg and places it forward without making the slightest ripple. He imperceptibly raises his head. Then, suddenly, in one great lightning stroke, the long sharp bill viciously strikes the water. The victim, a squirming sculpin, slides headfirst down the heron's big throat, the sculpin's bony fins scraping the gullet and making the downward slide difficult for the heron which emits a hoarse guttural sound, and then awkwardly takes flight.

He flies low along the shoreline, with slow deep wing beats, the long neck doubled back on the shoulders and legs trailing. One of our largest resident birds, the Great Blue Heron reaches 1.5 meters in height and has a wingspread of nearly 2 meters. In summer these large bluish-gray birds wear breeding plumage: a white head with black side stripes, yellowish bill, long blackish legs, streaked grayish-brown neck, long plumes on the lower neck and back. In winter the plumes disappear. Herons are frequently mistaken for cranes, but in flight the heron's long neck is doubled back, U-shaped; the neck of the Sandhill Crane is fairly stretched out. Herons frequent protected coastal bays and estuaries as well as fresh-water ponds, marshes, and streams. They prefer fish, but also take crustaceans, frogs, salamanders, insects, and small mammals.

Great Blue Heron
summer plumage

A flock of several dozen high-flying birds with necks held straight out and long yellow legs trailing spiral down to land on the mud flat, the Greater Yellowlegs, *Tringa melanoleuca*. These hungry travelers run rapidly about the muddy shore or wade thigh high for crustaceans and aquatic insects. The Greater Yellowlegs is one of our best known shorebirds, living exclusively in shallow water areas lined with grasses, rushes, and cattails on both the outer coast and on inland lakes. These large graceful waders have dark gray and white checkered mantles, speckled necks and chest, whitish below-tail, barred whitish tails, and long slender dark bills slightly upturned. A smaller version of the Greater Yellowlegs, the Lesser Yellowlegs, *Tringa flavipes*, (not pictured) is about one quarter smaller and has a perfectly straight bill; the Greater has a clear, three-note whistle, "whew, whew, whew", while the Lesser has a two-note whistle, "you, you". Both birds nod and teeter on their long bright yellow legs. Both appear during their spring and fall migration, but under favorable conditions some of both species winter on our coast.

Greater Yellowlegs

Another cluster of shorebirds wading belly high in the nearby shallows probes the bottom for worms, crustaceans, fish eggs, tiny snails, and clams. The Long-billed Dowitchers, *Limnodromus scolopaceus*, rapidly dunk their heads in and out like sewing machine needles when feeding, and are so absorbed that they seldom panic when approached. Spring birds have brick-red throats, breasts, and underparts, and speckled reddish-brown mantles; winter birds have dull gray backs and breasts and white underparts. A distinctive field mark year round is the white below-tail and lower back. Long-billed Dowitchers migrate along the coast, stopping on salt water flats and grassy areas above beach to feed and rest. They are not common, but they are regular visitors, moving northward in April and passing back through from August to October. They often keep company with Short-billed Dowitchers, *Limnodromus griseus*, (not pictured). The two species look identical, though the Short-billed is a shade shorter and has a slightly smaller bill.

Long-billed Dowitcher
summer plumage

Mallard (male)

Mallard (female)

Canada Goose

Several pairs of resident shorebirds, the familiar Mallards, *Anas platyrhynchos*, waddle lazily on the mud bank or loaf and preen their feathers in the shallows. The females gabble continuously to the males in a low determined "quack quack", but the males tend to be silent, only occasionally giving a low pitched "kwek". The males cannot be mistaken: beautiful, iridescent green heads; white neck rings and outer tail feathers; chestnut lower necks and breasts; violet wing patches, yellowish bills, and orange legs. The females are dull: dark brown, speckled bodies; paler on the underparts; and a bright sky-blue patch with white bars on the edge of the wings. Mallards are wary, but highly adaptable, adjusting to almost any locale. In the wilds they feed primarily on vegetable matter or, during spawning season, on dead and dying salmon. In cultivated areas they feed regularly in farmers' fields on barley, wheat, and new shoots. Mallards are prolific, having eight to ten young, and using the entire Northwest, Central Canada, and Southwest Alaska as their breeding grounds. They breed readily with Pintails, Shovellers, and Black Ducks, and are the original stock from which our domestic varieties sprang.

A faint wild honking drifts over the mud flat, grows louder and finally appears as a great flying V — the Canada Geese, *Branta canadensis*. With powerful wing beats the heavily built birds move swiftly toward the flat, then glide gracefully down on set wings. The flock settles in to feed on tender aquatic roots as one or two sentinels keep watch, ready to give a warning call at the first sign of danger. The males and females dress alike: black head and neck, conspicuous white cheek patches, gray-brown upperparts, lighter underparts, black-tipped tail, and black bill and legs. Paired birds keep close together, so devoted to one another that should one be injured or killed the other frequently stays behind to risk the same fate. Large numbers spend the winter in coastal marshes, wildlife refuges, and in farmers' fields; others migrate along the length of the coast, from Mexico to Alaska. Because they are so clannish they tend to interbreed, and each isolated population differs somewhat in size, shape, and color. In fact, six subspecies of Canada Geese occur in the Pacific Northwest, all having black heads and necks and white cheek patches.

Black Brant

Where beds of bright green eelgrass glisten in the sun, the trim Black Brants, *Branta bernicla*, dine on succulent roots and stems. Their gullets filled, these dark geese gather on sandbars offshore to swallow grit, the roughage which helps them digest their meal. Small geese, they weigh up to 2.5 kg (6 pounds). The sexes are colored alike: black head, neck, and breast; smokey brown back and belly; white neck band, and whitish tail and below-tail. Brants breed farther north than any other geese, as far as Greenland, traveling low over the water, strung out in swift moving, rippling lines. The southward migration passes well out to sea, though a few small flocks do come down the inside passage. The bulk of the population arrives by mid-November and winters in scattered groups off the coastline from British Columbia to California. In early spring they begin to move steadily northward, this time stopping close to shore at sheltered salt bays and estuaries along the way. Brants are strictly marine birds: eelgrass makes up a large percentage of their food and without it most of them would disappear.

A raft of slate-gray bodies with whitish, chicken-like bills rides high in open water, making harsh "kacks, clucks, and coos" at one another, the American Coots, *Fulica americana*. Belonging to the rail family, coots may as well be ducks: their long lobed toes help them to swim and dive, and they tip headfirst to pick at the bottom or graze on shore. The American Coot dwells on marshy lakes and rivers over most of North America, often visiting golf courses and city parks for insects, snails, grasses, seeds, and aquatic plants. Large flocks winter along our Northwest coast, but during the breeding season move to inland ponds and marshes to anchor their floating, basket-like nests to shoreline cattails and tuberous roots. Because some chicks emerge before others the male parent takes the firstcomers into the marsh to feed while the female continues sitting. Nicknamed "mud hen", it prefers marshy, often muddy waters.

American Coot

A long, high pitched laugh echoes over the quiet shallows of the mud flat: the Common Loon, *Gavia immer*, calls to its mate. The birds work themselves into a vocal frenzy, sending yodeling cries far and wide to set off a chain of yodeling answers from across the bay. With their heavy bodies and short thick necks they ride low in the water; the legs are set so far back on the body that on land they are of little use for walking or standing. During the nesting season loons return to fresh-water lakes and ponds, usually one pair to a lake. The birds always try to go back to the same nest of mud, roots, and branches at the water's edge. Juveniles and winter adults have gray upperparts and white breasts, but both sexes dress in identical mating plumage: black head, neck and bill; black mantle checkered with white diamond-shapes and spots; white striped neck collar, and white underparts. The loons stand upright and race side by side over the water, then face each other to perform a strange, ritualistic dance. After courtship, the female lays two dark brown eggs spotted with black. When the young are ready to travel, the loons migrate to the seacoast. Later, a second migration occurs southward, but a large number of birds remains to forage along the seacoast during the winter.

Common Loon
summer plumage

The perky little Buffleheads, *Bucephala albeola*, ride high in the water, then dive deeply to the bottom to pick up food. While the flock dives sentries attentively ride the waves, ready to give a warning signal at the first sign of danger. Suddenly those at the surface rise abruptly from the water and the rest burst into the air, like flying missiles, from the depths below. The males are exceptionally striking: contrasting pure white crests set on black heads glossed with greenish-violet reflections; black mantles; white underparts; and large white wing patches. The females have well feathered large-appearing heads, hence the names "Buffalo Head", "Butter Ball", and "Bufflehead". They breed in scattered locations near suitable inland ponds and lakes. The female builds her nest in holes and trees and stumps or in burrows in the ground, and lays up to twelve ivory colored eggs. When inland autumn leaves turn golden Buffleheads gather into large flocks to feed on dead and dying salmon, but as the wind becomes increasingly cold, many fly south along the coastline, the rest remaining on the Northwest coast.

Bufflehead

Riding high in the water, the American Widgeon, *Anas americana*, tips for seaweeds or dabbles at the surface for floating plants. Ill-equipped for diving, the surface-feeding Widgeons wait for diving birds to bring up succulent seaweeds, then snatch the plants from the unsuspecting divers and in a spray of white water wildly swim away. The males are handsome ducks: generally creamy-gray speckled with black; snow-white breast and abdomen; pinkish-brown sides; white patches on the undersides of the wings, and green and black areas on the upper sides; black below-tail; bold glossy green patches through the eye; a conspicuous white forehead and cap inspired the name "Baldplate Widgeon". In comparison the females are dull, having brown bodies, gray heads, and white breasts. The breeding area extends throughout Oregon, Washington, British Columbia, central Alaska, and east to the Great Lakes, and they n⟋ ⁓mally breed inland and then migrate to the seacoast. Regular fall and spring migrants, they are the most conspicuous winter duck along the Pacific coastline to the Gulf of Mexico. Large numbers regularly visit coastal bays and nearby lakes, forage in farmers' fields for seeds or on newly seeded crops, or graze on the grass on golf courses or in parks.

American Widgeon

Near the entrance to the bay, in deeper water, a large flock of fast flying Greater Scaups, *Aythya marila*, skim to a landing and easily ride the choppy water. Even from a distance the color pattern of the males is distinct, black for the front half of the body and white for the back. The white-faced brown females trail after the drakes. Suddenly the muffled din of "scaup, scaup" rises from the group, then all dive at once to the bottom to feed on shellfish and eelgrass. The Greater Scaup is a common winter resident, but in spring migrates northward to build new nests of rushes and grasses in little hollows near fresh-water ponds. This species and the closely related Lesser Scaup, *Aythya affinis*, with their blue bills, are difficult to distinguish in the field, but the male Greater Scaup is slightly larger, has a whiter back, and a glossy green head and neck instead of the glossy blue as in the Lesser Scaup. Also the Greater Scaup has larger white stripes on the wings, particularly noticeable during flight. Both species are commonly called "bluebills".

Greater Scaup

179

Circling high overhead a pure white bird with a black cap silently searches the calm sheltered mud flat and looks for prey, the Common Tern, *Sterna hirundo*. So graceful is this slender gull-like bird with its pointed bill and long narrow wings extending beyond its deeply forked tail, that it is known as the "sea swallow". The bird suddenly drops from a considerable height and plunges head first into deep water, emerging within seconds amidst white spray and rising in a steep climb with a fish clamped in its bill. The small delicate-looking bird has a pearly-gray mantle, white tail and breast, black head-cap, dusky tail feathers, and bright orange-red feet and bill. In winter the black cap retreats to become a blackish patch at the back of the head, the red bill turns blackish, and the red legs fade. Common Terns visit the bays and harbors along our coast both in spring and fall, and rarely leave the ocean, but in winter they fly swiftly to Baja California, some flying all the way to the foot of South America, and in May return to their breeding range which extends from along the Atlantic coast to the Great Plains and to Alberta.

Common Tern

Immediately a wild nasal scream cuts the air. A hawk-like bird, the Parasitic Jaeger, *Stercorarius parasiticus*, swoops down to rob the tern of its fish, attacking fiercely with hooked beak and slashing claws. The speedy tern races to get away: diving, wheeling, and looping. But the hungry jaeger pursues. Finally, the tern drops the fish, the jaeger turns, snatches it in mid-air, and swallows it whole. Seen at a distance the Parasitic Jaeger is black and white with two pointed heavy protruding tail feathers and a peculiar hawk-like flight, but adult birds have two color phases, one light, one dark. In the light color phase the neck and underparts are white, the sides of the neck yellow, the upper parts gray, and the cap blue; in the dark phase the bird is brownish all over. All along our coast Parasitic Jaegers are common on mud flats and sandy beaches and rocky shores. In spring they move northward to their breeding grounds in the tundra, but travel far out to sea. In the fall they travel closer to shore, continuing their piracy by following migrant gulls, terns, and other fish-eating birds down the seacoast, and robbing them of their catch along the way.

Parasitic Jaeger

Look into the shallow pools of water at the very surface of soft mud, especially where silt and decaying seaweeds accumulate, to see the great hordes of tiny silvery Nebalia, *Nebalia pugettensis*, crustaceans only about 1 cm long, so tiny that they can live in those shallows until the tide returns. These odd little animals have an inflated carapace and a tiny head covered with a hard, helmet-like structure. The carapace and bristly legs create currents of water from which the animal strains diatoms and other decaying food particles.

Nebalia

Where muddy sand is very soft, particularly where covered with patches of Sea Lettuce, numerous active ribbon-like worms, the Mud Nemerteans, *Paranemertes peregrina*, crawl on their little slime trails at the surface — also called the Restless Worm. The smooth upper side of this thin fragile animal is dark brown or purplish-black; the underside, pale yellow; the head is semi-flattened and the tail pointed. It busily crawls along at the surface or swims in shallow water: strong muscular actions shorten and lengthen the body, the beating of the tiny hairs covering the body create a current. The nemertean injects poison into its prey — particularly worms — and, when the victim is quiet, swallows it whole.

Mud Nemertean

A crab found in firm mud and frequently in oyster beds is the Graceful Cancer Crab, *Cancer gracilis*. This light reddish-orange or grayish-tan crab is related to the Dungeness Crab and the Red Rock Crab, but the Graceful Cancer Crab has a smaller body, about 10 to 12 cm across the carapace; distinctly shaped notches on the front edge of its carapace, and a near-absence of hairs on the underside; and long, slender graceful walking legs and claws. This species is edible, but rarely taken because of its comparatively small size and because it rarely occurs abundantly.

Graceful Cancer Crab

In quiet bays where fresh water drains into the sea, oysters are usually common. Most species alternate in gender being either male or female from season to season or annually. A medium-sized female oyster may discharge half a million eggs into the water in one season, the male oyster gives off sperm, and fertilization occurs in the open water. The larvae freely swim about as plankton for a short time, then settle down on clam shells, rocks, or other hard surfaces, and most lose the ability to move.

Native Oyster

Occurring sporadically, our own Native Oyster, *Ostrea lurida*, adheres to rocks, the shell only 5 cm in length, generally gray externally and olive-green or grayish on the inside. This species is becoming increasingly rare, possibly because of pollution, temperature changes, or competition from other animals. This Native or "Olympia" Oyster is a delicious food cultivated to some extent in Puget Sound, but not extensively marketed because of its small size and dwindling populations.

On almost every type of protected beach the Japanese Oyster, *Crassostrea gigas*, reaches a length of 25 cm or more — a giant oyster — the gray or white shells smooth or highly irregular and fluted. The oyster is usually, but not always, cemented onto something hard like a rock or another oyster, and generally takes the shape of the object to which it is attached, a characteristic which accounts for the variety of shapes. The species is a newcomer to our coast: Japanese oyster spat, or "oyster seed", was originally imported from Japan in 1905 to be planted on our own native oyster beds, and is now so well established that the Pacific coast oyster industry is based almost entirely on it. People with oyster leases import spat to replace the harvested oysters because rarely are the Northwest waters warm enough to encourage spawning.

When shucking oysters on the beach, remember to leave the shells. The oyster larvae will attach and develop into a whole new crop.

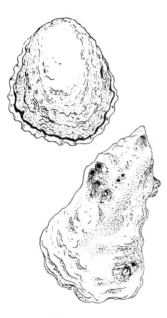

Japanese Oyster

An interesting mussel half buried at the surface, with only the tip of the shell protruding, the Horse Mussel, *Modiolus rectus*, is also called the Bearded Mussel because it attaches itself to buried rocks by its long byssal threads. It often forms aggregates by attaching to the shells of other mussels, the large, wedge-shaped shells being about 20 cm long and rounded at both ends. Young specimens tend to be shiny brown, older ones nearer blackish-brown. Like other mussels this one feeds by letting its shells gape slightly to filter microscopic food from the sea water that passes through the small and incomplete siphons. While Horse Mussels do occur intertidally, they occur only at the lowest tide levels and are more abundant in deeper water.

Horse Mussel

Occasionally a tiny bag-shaped figure hangs from oysters, rocks, and empty clam shells — even from discarded tin cans — the Hairy Sea Squirt, *Boltenia villosa*. The body is covered with numerous little hairs, and water squirts out of the openings at the top when the animal is squeezed: a dirty orange or bright red; the hairs a muddy brown. The size varies considerably, but a height of 3 cm is common. They are filter feeders straining microscopic food from currents of sea water that pass through the siphon-like openings at the top. Because sea squirts attach by a very distinct tough stalk to any kind of solid objects, they can be found on a wide variety of places including rocky shores and on oyster flats.

Hairy Sea Squirt
Photo 61 p. 36

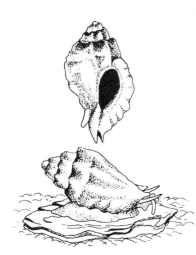

Along with Japanese Oysters came an unwelcome newcomer to our shores, the Oyster Drill, _Ocenebra japonica_, a serious pest which uses its specialized radula to rasp a neat little hole through the shells of oysters and other shellfish in order to eat the soft flesh inside. The Oyster Drill is difficult to distinguish from the Rock Whelk of the rocky shore, but the shell of the Oyster Drill is always frilly whereas the shell of the Rock Whelk varies considerably, being frilly when exposed to the open sea and quite smooth in quieter waters such as those containing oyster beds. Since 1947 the Japanese have been inspecting all exported oyster spat to prevent the continued spread of Oyster Drills and other associated pests. The only way to control the Oyster Drill locally is to pick them from oyster beds by hand.

Oyster Drill

Quiet bays, particularly those with brackish surface water, often have the Black Dog Whelk, _Nassarius obsoletus_, a short, plump, well camouflaged snail, its smooth shell and dull black color enabling it to blend into its dark habitat. Reaching a height of 2.5 cm, the Black Dog came to the west coast along with oyster spat from the Atlantic, and like the dreaded Oyster Drill is at times a predator, but fortunately it is also a scavenger and seems to cause little damage to oyster beds.

Black Dog Whelk

Sometimes in a shallow bay with a bottom of firm mud mixed with sand are vast numbers of small Screw Shells, _Batillaria attramentaria_, the long spiral shells about 2.5 cm in length. Though similar to that of the Threaded Horn Snails of the rocky shores, the shell of the Screw Shells have dark brown "beads" that create attractive spiral bands across a field of gray. Like the Oyster Drill, Screw Shells were accidentally imported from Japan along with the Japanese Oysters, but do not appear to be serious predators.

Screw Shell

Occasionally an absurd-looking creature something like a large and grotesque reddish dill pickle becomes stranded on the rocks or in sandy or muddy flats when the tide drops, the California Sea Cucumber, *Parastichopus californicus*. When undisturbed this giant among sea cucumbers stretches out to its full 40 to 45 cm, but when annoyed contracts to 15 to 20 cm and becomes very firm. It has a tough, reddish-brown or orangish-brown skin covered with many large warts, and rows of tube feet on the underside of the body used for attaching and moving, and fifteen mop-like branched tentacles about the mouth. When severely disturbed the California Sea Cucumber spews out its internal organs, gut tract, respiratory tree, stomach and all. But consider this: while its predator is busily helping itself to a few appetizing items, the sea cucumber itself slowly steals away, and then grows a new and complete set of internal organs.

California Sea Cucumber
Photo 59 p. 35

In shallow muddy waters, under algae and especially among small pebbles, the tiny Small Brittle Star, *Amphipholis squamata*, a writhing, snake-like figure, reaches a total width of only 3 cm. Dull in color, usually gray above and whitish underneath, the Small Brittle Star feeds mainly on diatoms and microscopic plants. Handle this sea star carefully: the five very slender rays are fragile.

Small Brittle Star

Heart Cockle
Photo 25 p. 24

Several species of clams live buried beneath the surface of muddy, sandy, or cobbley beaches. Most of them feed during high tides by pumping water in through the "in" siphon and through the gills where they filter out the food; they then pump the water and body wastes out through the "out" siphon. Clams feed on microscopic plankton as well as on detritus and bacteria: a few species extract food particles directly from surface mud. Occasionally a one-celled planktonic organism called *Gonyaulax* becomes so numerous that it colors the water: hence "red tide". When filter-feeding shellfish, such as clams, mussels, oysters, and scallops feed on *Gonyaulax*, the shellfish itself is not harmed, but toxin concentrates in the internal organs may become toxic to humans. However, *Gonyaulax* does not cause all red tides, and not all shellfish become toxic to the same extent. In fact, after a *Gonyaulax* tide all shellfish become nontoxic within four to six weeks, with the exception of the Butter Clam which may remain toxic for two years or more. Rarely do shellfish become toxic enough in our waters to cause illness, and then mainly during the summer on beaches close to the open ocean. Fisheries officials and Health authorities do keep a check on the presence of paralytic shellfish poisoning, nevertheless, and post bulletins on wharves, in post offices, and on marinas.

In quiet bays where deposits of mud and sand build up around the rocks, and in eelgrass flats, there is a rather striking clam, the Heart Cockle, *Clinocardium nuttallii*. When viewed from either end, the valves have a heart-shaped profile; the two 10 cm shells are equal, each one being thick and heavy with strong ribs running up and down from the hinge. Young specimens are pale yellow and mottled; older specimens, reddish-brown. This clam sits on the bottom or burrows beneath the surface: the short siphons restrict it to shallow burrows, and when approached by predators the foot enables it to dig rapidly. Observe this amazing digging activity by placing one of them in a pan of sea water, or a tidepool, and watching the cockle push itself around. Place the arm of a Sunflower Sea Star beside the clam: the cockle will react violently and try to escape; it may even flip over.

Fairly high on the beach, where fresh-water seepage washes muddy sand or muddy gravel, the Mud Clam burrows, *Mya arenaria*. Often called the Soft-shelled Clam because of its thin brittle shells — which clam diggers usually crack — it is basically chalky-white with a thin layer of yellow or brown skin at the edges. The size varies considerably, but a shell length of 10 to 15 cm is common. The clam has a spoon-shaped tooth in the left valve of the interior hinge, and an elongated siphon which allows the clam to live 20 to 35 cm below the surface of flats. Discarded Mud Clam shells do not occur in our west coast Indian middens because the clam was introduced to our waters about fifty years ago from the east coast.

Mud Clam

A clam that burrows in muddy sand, often in brackish or polluted water, the Bent-nosed Clam, *Macoma nasuta*, takes its name from the shape of the shells which bend sharply like a nose. The small thin chalky-white shells rarely exceed 5 cm in length. Its orange colored and divided siphons, and its bent shape, distinguish this clam from similar species. A food delicacy, but very small.

Bent-nosed Clam

Another small clam in similar locations, the Macoma Clam, *Macoma irus*, is about the size of and looks like the Bent-nosed Clam, but its shells are not bent, the hinge ligament is large and prominent, and the siphons are pale yellow, not at all orange. Both would be quite edible except for their small size and their "sloppy" food gathering which brings excessive sand inside the shells. The presence of both the Bent-nosed Clam and the Macoma Clam indicate low oxygen levels in the mud and water and may indicate surface pollution.

Macoma Clam

On mixed mud and sand, look for a pile of fine sand and gravel around a little hole about the diameter of a pencil. The hole leads down to an intriguing slow-moving creature called the Ghost Shrimp, *Callianassa californiensis*, appropriately named because its soft delicate body, up to 8 or 9 cm long, is pinkish-orange or pinkish-gray on top and paler underneath. In spite of its helpless appearance the industrious Ghost Shrimp spends its time building elaborate burrows complete with turn around chambers and at least two openings to the surface. It feeds on detritus, including bacteria, which it extracts from the continuous stream of mud passing through its digestive tract.

Ghost Shrimp

A sea anemone living subtidally in soft mud or in soft muddy sand, the Tube-dwelling Anemone, *Pachycerianthus fimbriatus*, has a yellowish or brownish oral disc with nearly transparent or whitish tentacles showing pink cross bands near the base. Unlike other anemones, this one lacks a pedal disc, but forms a long, parchment-like tube of sand grains, shell fragments, and similar debris, bound together by a sticky mucous and covering the entire column up to the tentacles. When disturbed the animal defends itself by rapidly withdrawing deep into its tube which may extend 50 to 75 cm below the surface. They have two circles of tentacles; an outer circle of extremely long ones and an inner circle of short ones. When the animal moves up to the surface, the long graceful tentacles sweep a wide area for food and bring it to the small ones which carry the food into the mouth.

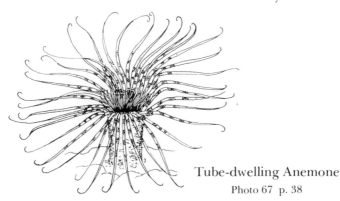

Tube-dwelling Anemone
Photo 67 p. 38

In habitats even muddier than those of the Ghost Shrimp, the Mud Shrimp, *Upogebia pugettensis*, digs its permanent and very deep U-shaped living burrows as far down as 60 cm with two openings 60 to 90 cm apart. When burrowing the Mud Shrimp uses its extremely large flattened claws as scoops for digging, and carries its mud in a "basket" formed by stiff hairs located along the inside of the claws. The swimming legs and the tail flap act as paddles to keep the water circulating through the burrow. As the water circulates the first two pairs of legs strain detritus and other food particles from the water through the fine hairs covering the legs. The Mud Shrimp occasionally inhabits the same flat as the Ghost Shrimp, but the Mud Shrimp is generally hairy, pale grayish-brown or whitish, and has a larger, firmer body; its burrows do not have the little piles of sand and fine gravel at the surface.

Mud Shrimp
Photo 10 p. 20

Turn the Mud Shrimp upside down to see the small clam that attaches itself to the underside of the Mud Shrimp's abdomen, the Mud Shrimp Clam, *Pseudopythina rugifera*, about 1 cm. This unusual clam spins a byssus something like the threads of mussels in order to anchor itself to its host, enjoys the protection of a burrow, and filters microscopic food from the water that the shrimp circulates through the burrow.

Mud Shrimp Clam

In mud and muddy sand there will almost always be several species of burrowing segmented worms. One common species leaves numerous fine blackish castings at the surface, the Thread Worm, *Notomastus tenuis*, an extremely long and slender dark red worm, 1 mm wide and 20 to 30 cm long. They have very tiny bristly feet on each side of most segments, are extremely slender, have two dark patches or "eye spots" on the first segment, and no tentacles on the head. In some places Thread Worms are so plentiful that a shovel full of mud may reveal a hundred or so specimens; however, most of these will be broken because their long slender bodies are extremely fragile. Thread Worms digest detritus and decaying plant and animal matter in the mud passing through their bodies.

Thread Worm

Tubes of sand sticking a little above the surface of hard-packed muddy sand likely belong to dull reddish Bamboo Worms, *Axiothella rubrocincta*, 15 to 18 cm in length. They have long slim fragile bodies and their segments are longer than wide and swollen at the joints, much like a stick of bamboo. Remove intact by carefully digging down with a shovel and then picking the mud away by hand.

Bamboo Worm

On almost any protected bay, notice the numerous coiled castings on the surface — like mud pressed through a cake decorator. Dig down around the castings to discover large populations of Lugworms, *Abarenicola pacifica*, with their tapering, segmented bodies. Generally of a drab yellowish-brown or greenish-brown, or pinkish color. The worm excavates U-shaped burrows of sufficient size that both ends of the animal almost reach the surface. As the worm digs it digests food particles from the mud passing through the gut, the leftover mud and debris passing out of the body to form the coiled fecal castings at the surface.

Lugworm

Buried below the low tide line in mud and sand is a worm so beautiful that it is called after Aphrodite, the Greek goddess of beauty: the deceptive Sea Mouse, *Aphrodita japonica*. When muddy it looks like a long bristly mottled slug, but when washed the Sea Mouse turns out to be quite glorious. The underside of the 10 to 15 cm body is divided into equal segments, each with a pair of paddle-like feet tipped with bristles, and reveals the animal to be a scaleworm. Fine short hairs cover the upper side, and two rows of long metallic bristles run around the margins reflecting gold, scarlet, red, or orange. The Sea Mouse feeds on detritus and on other slow moving worms.

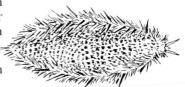

Before leaving the mud flats remember to fill in the holes.

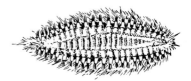

Sea Mouse

98 Sea Lettuce on a cobblestone beach near Courtenay, Vancouver Island, B.C.

The Cobblestone Beach

The entrance to a cobblestone beach. A winding dirt path over a treeless, barren hillside, a fresh-water stream meandering gracefully to the bay and cutting through a gravel bank to reveal empty clam shells — an Indian midden, one of the many places along our coast where Native Indians camped and made their meals on the bounty from the sea. Judging from the contents of the midden, Butter Clams, Little-neck Clams, Cockles, and Horse Clams were important as food, jewelry, and trade items. The rich black soil has been fertilized by the decayed remains of clams.

Do not confuse protected cobblestone beaches with those gravel beaches on rocky headlands, or those on islands facing southward, or those on the exposed outer coast. On that outer coast the strong wave action continuously tumbles stones until they become pulverized gravel, pebbles, and sand. Among the beautifully rounded stones of such beaches are countless polished gems: jet-black, mossy-green, milky-white, steel-gray, and melon-yellow. But those gravel beaches of the outer coast are a wasteland: few, if any, animals can survive the harsh abrasive action of constantly tumbling rocks.

But here on a cobblestone beach protected by the inlet and the bay, the wave action is much less. The beaches are very different: the stones are smooth and round and much larger, often between 10 to 30 cm in diameter. The stream deposits loose gravel mixed with sand and mud, and because the wave action is not great enough to carry the mixture out to sea, mixed sand and mud provides a stable bottom for plants and animals. On some beaches the tops of cobblestones teem with life, but the abrasive action of sand moved by water polishes the sides and bottom edges clean.

Above Beach

Many plants and animals living here are associated with rocky shores, particularly in the higher zones where the rocks are covered with hordes of little black periwinkles, thousands of barnacles and mussels, and the usual collection of snails and limpets. On some cobblestone beaches, in the upper zones, bright green Sea Lettuce and Sea Hair cover the rocks, on other cobblestone beaches the rockweeds completely predominate. Beneath the cobblestones and boulders the shore crabs hide and the little clingfish and blennies slither into holes and crevices when the tide drops. There are no sculpins here because the sand and mud and gravel mixture makes too loose a bottom to hold permanent pools of water.

But under the cobblestones that very mixture provides a loose, coarse bottom for such animals as clams and worms that can burrow easily. In fact some cobblestone beaches have so many clams and are so strewn with empty clam shells that they are known as "shell beaches". The clams burrow to a depth limited by the length of their siphons; thus some species — and the young of most species — are close to the surface, while other species burrow deep down. In some places specialized burrowing sea cucumbers and anemones attach to rocks below the surface and only the tentacles protrude.

In most bays, because the combination of cobblestone, gravel, sand, and mud changes so gradually that particular conditions tend to overlap, do not be surprised to turn up plants and animals more commonly associated with rocky shores, muddy flats, or even sandy beaches. On our coastline, cobblestone, or "mixed" beaches, frequently appear along the protected shores of Puget Sound and along the inland passage of the Straits of Georgia.

A small and frequently abundant anemone living in sand or gravel on semi-protected cobblestone or rocky shores, the Green Burrowing Anemone, *Anthopleura artemisia*, grows up to 2 or 3 cm in diameter with tentacles which may spread to 8 cm. It attaches by a long and narrow column to rocks or shells, 15 to 20 cm below the surface, and only the oral disc and tentacles protrude, the tentacles a dull gray to olive or dark green with occasionally light bands. The upper part of the stalk is generally coarse and covered with sand or bits of broken shell, the lower part cream colored and quite smooth. Occasionally solitary specimens attach to cobblestones at the surface and have short thick stalks.

Buried in coarse sand, gravel, and shell debris, with only the disc and tentacles showing, the Red-beaded Anemone, *Tealia coriacea*, grows to about half the size of the Giant Green Anemone, 5 to 10 cm in diameter. The handsome Red-beaded has short stubby red and gray tentacles with bright cross bands, its exceptionally thick and bright crimson column often has yellow stripes or blotches, and is invariably covered with pebbles or shell fragments; the foot attaches firmly to rocks below the surface.

Green Burrowing
Anemone
Photo 75 p. 41

Red-beaded Anemone
Photo 70 p. 40

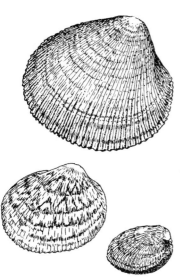

Native Little-neck Clam

Japanese
Little-neck Clam

The soft mud and sand deposits under cobbles and boulders support large populations of clams. To dig for them look for a number of holes at the surface: when the tide drops the clams withdraw their siphons. Use a three-pronged long-handled fork or shovel. Small clams will re-bury, but may not survive large amounts of gravel being turned over. Check for and follow the legal limits set for each species; these regulations change from year to year depending on local clam populations. Follow the legal limits strictly: many clam beds are rapidly becoming depleted because of greedy diggers. As a general rule take the first clams you dig, regardless of species, and take away all broken clams regardless of size.

One abundant species on firm gravel-mud is the Native Little-neck Clam, *Protothaca staminea*, its medium-sized shell reaching about 6 cm. The two fairly thick and strong valves have fine ridges running up and down and across the surface, crisscrossing it. Adult specimens tend to be evenly light brown, sometimes a little pinkish; younger specimens tend to be marked with chocolate-brown designs looking like little triangles or little checker boards; the inside of the shell is white with a deep purple blotch. The Native Little-neck usually occurs near the surface in great numbers — quite edible and at one time the most important commercial clam on our coast.

A similar clam also lives in shallow burrows in muddy sand but slightly higher on the beach, the gray or light brown Japanese Little-neck Clam, *Venerupis japonica*. Frequently juveniles show intriguing dark brown geometric designs. This species is similar in length to the Native Little-neck — 5 to 6 cm — but the Japanese Little-neck is more pleasing to look at because of its distinct oblong shape. Accidentally introduced into our Northwest waters along with the Japanese Oysters, the Japanese Little-neck has increased in numbers so rapidly that it is now more abundant than the Native Little-neck. It too is quite edible, marketed in large numbers and generally steamed open. Both these relatively small Little-necks are often called "steamer clams".

On sandy or cobbley beaches and usually in mixtures of porous broken shell and gravel, the fairly large Butter Clam, *Saxidomus giganteus*, reaches a length of 10 to 12 cm. The thick oval-to-square shells are quite heavy, with prominent concentric lines: the adult shell generally grayish-white, not glossy, and often slightly blackish because of sulphur dioxide in the sand; the young shell, generally yellowish. Butter Clam shells have a large prominent brownish or blackish hinge ligament. Butter Clams frequent the lower third of tidal regions and the deeper waters. They are delicious in clam chowder, and because of their numbers and large size they are the most important commercial clam in the Northwest.

Butter Clam

Deep below the surface of muddy sand and gravel in a semi-permanent burrow lives the Geoduck Clam, *Panope generosa*, the largest clam on our coast, in fact one of the largest burrowing bivalves in the world. Its body parts are so large, up to 3 or 4.5 kg (6 or 10 pounds), that the animal cannot withdraw them completely into its heavy shells which therefore gape widely. The grayish-white and nearly rectangular shells with their rough concentric lines may reach 20 cm or more in length, but 12 to 15 cm is most common. Look at them from above. The immense light brown siphons extend upward to the surface. The only other similar siphons are those of the Horse Clam, but the siphons of the Geoduck do not have leather-like flaps on the tips. The inexperienced clam digger often digs down only part way and then tries to pull the Geoduck out by the siphons, thinking the clam to be hanging on with stubborn determination or trying to dig deeper. But the embattled clam, as deep as 1 or 2 meters, could not surrender itself even if it wanted to: the siphons are not strong enough for dragging the bulging body through the wet and muddy sand. Should the siphons break, continue to dig around the clam and take it up. Otherwise, the clam will die anyway.

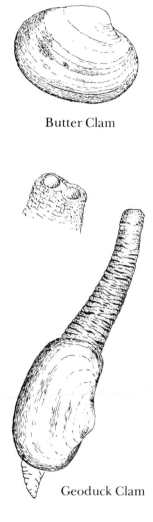

Geoduck Clam

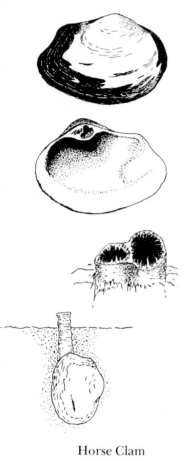

Where mud, sand, or gravel, and pieces of broken shell mix together, look for water shooting like fountains a meter or so high. Deep below the surface the large Horse Clams, *Tresus capax*, retract their siphons. Variously known as Rubberneck Clams, Gaper Clams, Washington Clams, Blue Clams, and Horse Clams, this species may reach 20 cm in length and may weigh as much as 1.5 kg (3 or 4 pounds). Unless discolored, the shells are chalky-white or yellowish; generally smooth with concentric lines and covered with a thin brown skin which peels easily. The long leathery siphon is covered by a wrinkled, rubbery skin; the tip covered with a leathery flap on which algae, barnacles, and anemones often grow. The Horse Clam generally lives at some depth, usually not less than 30 cm, and sometimes as deep as 75 to 100 cm. Quite edible, but as yet not used commercially because digging usually breaks the shells and the meat dries out. Diggers generally think the species is not so tasty as others, and leave the Horse Clams on the surface where they die because they cannot rebury themselves. Dig for Horse Clams, but take them home and cook them, grinding up the meat before cooking. If you don't want them, be sure to rebury them at the same depth because the animal relies on the pressure of the sand to hold its spring-hinge ligament together.

Horse Clam

Open a Horse Clam. Almost every one will have at least one pair of soft-bodied Pea Crabs living inside, *Pinnixa faba*, each about 1.5 cm across the carapace. These crabs live in pairs, a male and a female, the female generally the larger. By living inside the clam, Pea Crabs have a protected house and food from the sea water brought in through the clam's siphons. The Pea Crab is one of many species of small commensal crabs living in harmless association with clams.

Pea Crab

The under-rock habitat on cobblestone beaches protects an assortment of fairly specialized worms, including the Green Ribbon Worm of the rocky shore and the Sand Worm of the sandy beach. Another worm building its own "home" from fragments of shell and stone and other debris is the Hairy Gilled Worm, *Thelepus crispus*, up to 15 cm long with 60 to 90 segments. Three pairs of long red gills and numerous long pink prey-catching tentacles extend from the head end. The Hairy Gilled Worm belongs to a family of tube builders that cements hard particles together with a sticky mucus to form a protective tube-like house up to 30 cm long and .5 cm wide. When disturbed this worm simply leaves its tube and builds a new one in another location.

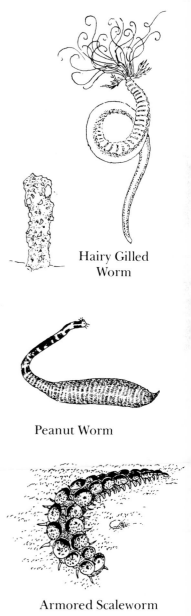

Hairy Gilled Worm

Under rocks where sandy mud and gravel accumulate there is a muscular non-segmented worm called the Peanut Worm, *Phascolosoma agassizii*. When contracted it becomes very firm and takes on the shape of a shelled peanut, but when extended it becomes much more slender. Not a true worm, it has no segments or bristles, but a body surface with a tough, wrinkled skin; the plump head end drab tan or greenish-tan; and the tail end pale with a number of black blotches. A Peanut Worm feeding at the surface uses the minute tentacles around its mouth to gather detritus and suspended food particles.

Peanut Worm

Strange armored worms crawl under rocks, around the holdfasts of seaweeds, and in mussel beds, the Armored Scaleworms, *Halosydna brevisetosa*. Eighteen pairs of mottled over-lapping grayish-brown scales are arranged in two longitudinal rows along the upper surface; the plates are easily lost but regenerate quickly. Other scaleworms live commensally with keyhole limpets, sea cucumbers, and sea stars. For example, one worm often hitches rides from the Mottled Star and benefits by helping itself to whatever the Mottled Star eats.

Armored Scaleworm

Turn the rocks back over, fill in the holes, put the animals back in their own habitats, or cover them with protective seaweed.

Exposed, Protected, and Transitional Shores

The irregularity of the Pacific coastline creates a variety of shores: exposed shores that take the full force of the beating waves, protected shores that receive little wave action, and transitional shores that are neither completely protected nor completely exposed to the hazards and surf-swept conditions of the open coast.

Exposed Shores

An outer coast completely exposed to the full force of beating surf has no offshore reefs, islands, or even kelp beds to provide protection from strong currents or violent wave action. Beaches here support a highly specialized but limited assortment of species because the plants and animals on an exposed shore must have special equipment with which to withstand the pounding surf and to prevent their being dislodged and carried away by strong currents. Exposed beaches are predominantly unprotected; and with sandy, gravelly, and rocky shores, or bold headlands.

Protected Shores

Protected shores are "protected" because they have offshore islands to shelter them, or bays and inlets to provide shelter from the full force of waves. On protected shores, sand and gravel bluffs tower above the coastline — they could not long survive on the outer coast. Typically, at the high tide line, protected beaches are often composed of cobblestones and gravel, and, at the low tide line, of sand.

These sheltered bays and muddy estuaries are comparatively rich in plants and animals which are out of danger from the waves and strong currents. In addition, because a sheltered beach of fine sand or mud retains water it provides a moist habitat for microscopic diatoms and for decaying plant and animal matter, the food of many larger animals.

Transitional Shores

Transitional shores are frequently dangerous and people seem to think that danger only lurks on the outer exposed coasts. The terms "exposed" and "protected" are relative and in certain places the calm sea can suddenly become violent and suddenly change shores that at first seemed "protected" into shores that are dangerously "exposed". Because most winter storms come from the south, coastlines with a southerly exposure are less protected than those facing in a northerly direction. Some organisms that live on exposed shores cannot live here because the transitional shore is often too calm. Others that live on the protected shores cannot live here because of the frequent violence. Transitional sand and gravel beaches are typically sterile places because of the scouring action of moving sand and gravel, but the cracks, crevices, and tidepools on transitional rocky shores house a wide assortment of rocky shore animals.

Exposed, Protected, and Transitional Shores

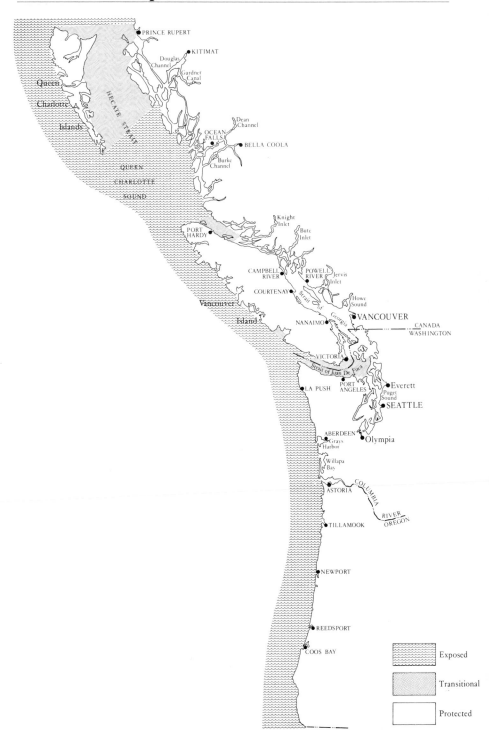

Headlands

99 Fog-shrouded Devil's Elbow, Yahats, Ore., is a basalt headland exposed to the full fury of violent surf.

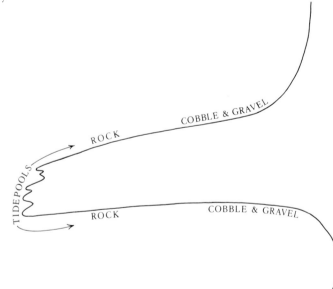

Headlands usually consist of rocks more resistant to erosion than the beaches on either side. Tidepools frequently occur at the base of the cliff. Depending on the strength of the offshore current there will be gravel or boulders on one side and frequently on both sides. Because of the constantly tumbling rocks these boulder and gravel beaches generally have no large intertidal plants and animals.

100 The sandspit at Dungeness Spit, Wa. extends for seven miles into the Strait of Juan de Fuca.

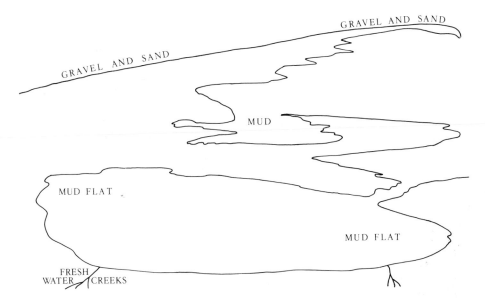

A spit is formed when offshore currents deposit sand and gravel where a shoreline changes direction. The spit which develops parallel to the natural coast is attached to one end, and creates an embayment into which rivers and streams deposit mud. Such tidal estuaries frequently produce a variety of bay clams.

101 The Olympic Peninsula, Wa.: the land once extended beyond the farthest remnants.

102 Sea stacks on the exposed Olympic Peninsula, Wa.

103 Sculptured trees: a sure sign of a wind and surf swept shore, near Bamfield, B.C.

104 Rich in seashore plants and animals: the tidepools and surge channels at Botany Bay, Port Renfrew, B.C.

105 Honeycombed surfaces of tilted sandstone and mudstone at Shore Acres, Cape Arago, Ore.

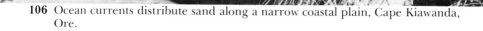

106 Ocean currents distribute sand along a narrow coastal plain, Cape Kiawanda, Ore.

107 The *Peter Iredale*, near Clatsop Spit, Ore., one of the many boats that strayed too close to a surf-swept shoreline.

108 Beach grasses, scotch broom, and sturdy beach pines help stabilize Dunes National Seashore, central Oregon.

109 Unstable sand dunes migrate inland, cover trees, and fill lakes at Dunes National Seashore, Ore.

110 Too hostile for seashore plants and animals: the abrasive moving sand, gravel, and cobble at surf-swept Ruby Beach, Wa.

111 Boulders and cobbles become trapped, tumbled, and rounded at crescent-shaped Yaquina Head Beach, Ore.

112 The gravel at Clallam Lighthouse, Wa., faces in a northerly direction into the Strait of Juan de Fuca: almost no surf during the summer, moderately protected in winter, and occasionally pounded by violent winter storms.

113 The sandy beach at San Juan Bay, Port Renfew, B.C : exposed to swift tidal currents between the open sea and the bay.

209

114 A protected rocky shoreline at Beaver Point, Salt Spring Island, B.C., a safe place with a rich assortment of plants and animals.

115 The cobblestone beach at Copper Cove, near Horseshoe Bay, B.C., with spectacular fiords in the distance.

116 Fanny Bay, Vancouver Island, B.C.: gravel at the high tide line, a broad sandy beach at the low tide line.

117 The many miles of mixed sand and mud tidal flats at Tillamook Bay, Ore.

The Oregon Coastline

Most of the 400 miles of Oregon coastline belong to the people of Oregon. U.S. highway 101 extends the full length of it, winding beside broad sandy beaches, sand dunes, sheltered coves, and rocky headlands, and dozens and dozens of state parks and waysides providing convenient access to the ocean. In addition, when completed in the early 1980's, a new foot trail will follow the path of early day travellers and provide a "close-up" of the varied and spectacular scenery.

The North Coast

The north coast lies between Astoria, at the mouth of the Columbia River, and Lincoln City. Wind-swept sandy beaches are typical and, where an unhampered surf rolls in, Razor Clams dig themselves in rapidly. Paralleling the shoreline is a sand dune area several miles wide, the result of sediments from the Columbia having been washed out to sea, carried in a southerly direction, and washed ashore again by ocean currents. A combination of exposed sandy beach, rocky headland, boulders, and bedrock appears at Ecola Point; sea stacks, needles, and arches, at Cannon Beach. There are miles and miles of mud flats which produce Heart Cockles, Butter Clams, Little-necks and Horse Clams at Tillamook Bay.

Eventually the white sandy beaches and river estuaries are interrupted by massive headlands and adjoining rocky areas. To see surf-carved sea caves and a small sandy beach, hike through the forest to the lighthouse at the tip of the headland in Cape Meares State Park. Another rocky headland juts out more than two miles into the sea at Cape Lookout to provide a panoramic view of a wind-swept and surf-pounded coast. Visit the "marine gardens" on the south side of the Cape. A sandy beach at Camp Meriwether is scattered with boulders and has an unusually heavy algal growth and a varied population of sea stars. To the south, at a wild ridge known as Cascade Head, the forest clashes with the open ocean.

The Central Coast

The central coast lies between Lincoln City and Coos Bay, a beach comber's paradise. A steep trail in Boiler Bay State Park leads down to an area of flat bedrock, tide channels, and tidepools. And a combination of sandy beaches, boulders, and offshore rocks provides a safe recreation area at nearby Fogarty Creek.

.A narrow rock-lined channel separates the scenic harbor of Depoe Bay from the open sea. To the south the flat sandstone shelves and numerous tidepools lined with Surfgrass, Sea Lettuce, Purple Urchins, and Common Purple and Ochre Stars become a "marine garden" at Otter Rock. The tideflats at busy Newport on Yaquina Bay produce bay clams and Dungeness Crabs. The Oregon State University Coastal Research Center here displays a large collection of marine life and is open to the public.

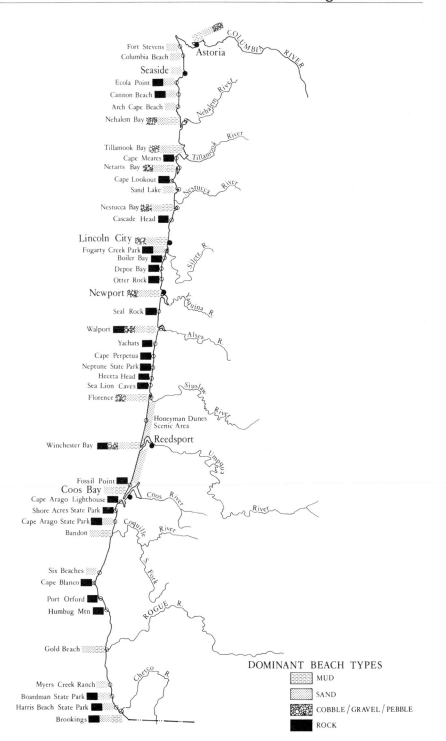

Fort Stevens
Columbia Beach
Astoria
COLUMBIA RIVER
Seaside
Ecola Point
Cannon Beach
Arch Cape Beach
Nehalem Bay
Nehalem River

Tillamook Bay
Cape Meares
Netarts Bay
Cape Lookout
Sand Lake
Tillamook River
Nestucca River
Nestucca Bay
Cascade Head

Lincoln City
Fogarty Creek Park
Boiler Bay
Depoe Bay
Otter Rock
Siletz R.
Newport
Yaquina R.
Seal Rock
Walport
Alsea R.
Yachats
Cape Perpetua
Neptune State Park
Heceta Head
Sea Lion Caves
Florence
Siuslaw River

Honeyman Dunes
Scenic Area
Winchester Bay
Reedsport
Umpqua River

Fossil Point
Coos Bay
Cape Arago Lighthouse
Shore Acres State Park
Cape Arago State Park
Bandon
Coos River
River
Coquille River

Six Beaches
Cape Blanco
S. Fork
Port Orford
Humbug Mtn
ROGUE R.

Gold Beach

Myers Creek Ranch
Boardman State Park
Harris Beach State Park
Brookings
Chetco R.

DOMINANT BEACH TYPES

MUD
SAND
COBBLE / GRAVEL / PEBBLE
ROCK

The Oregon Coastline

Southward a series of rugged headlands juts into crashing surf. A combination of cliffs, bedrock, boulders and offshore islands at Sea Rock gives some protection to the area, and to the usual collection of mussels, barnacles, sea stars, and seaweeds. But the presence of Sea Palms at Yachats State Park, with its exposed rocky shelf, indicates a hazardous surf-swept shore. At Cape Perpetua the magnificent basalt mountain created by several ancient lava flows drops abruptly into the sea where algal growth, mussel beds, sea stars, and anemones line surge channels and caves. The rocks are steep and the incoming tides hazardous at Neptune State Park on the southern boundaries of this Cape. And the wild sea surges over the black remains of another lava flow that has resisted erosion at Heceta Head.

The extensive dune area stretching fifty-four miles down this coast is designated the Oregon Dunes National Recreation Area, and extends from one to three miles inland. Vast, shifting, mountains of sand: wind-swept sand blown in an easterly direction creates islands of pine forest and, by blocking the flow of fresh-water streams, creates a string of warm coastal lakes just behind them.

The South Coast

At Coos Bay, the best natural harbor between Puget Sound and San Francisco Bay, recreational clam diggers and crabbers find easy access to tidelands. Because the coastline is rugged, Highway 101 winds its way often some distance from the water. From Coos Bay to Cape Arago, with its lighthouse overlooking eroding wave-cut rock, the shoreline is one of sandstone headlands. Sandstone cliffs protect Sunset Bay State Park from ocean winds while winter storms send huge bursts of white spray against those sculptured headlands at Shore Acres. Three coves break up popular Cape Arago State Park with its sandy beaches, tidepools and surge channels, and a variety of intertidal plants and animals — urchins, anemones, sea stars, corals, crabs, and seaweeds. A large intertidal area of relatively undisturbed sandy beaches, boulders, and fascinating tidepools, Cape Blanco is dangerous because of the incoming tides which often trap unwary visitors.

At the mouth of the Rogue River lies Gold Beach, and at Boardman State Park with its sand and pebble beach is a breathtaking view of rock arches covered by surf, and eroding dunes which extend to the edge of the bluff. The most southerly of Oregon's park campgrounds combines sandy beaches and dramatic offshore rocks: Harris Beach.

South of Coos Bay there are few towns and fewer picnic and camping sites, and access to the sea is more difficult. But the secluded beaches offer spectacular walks, and one of the greatest pleasures in driving the narrow roads that wind along the barren hillsides of the region is looking for miles out across the open sea to those rock arches and to those sea rocks which in the distance look like enormous sleeping sea lions.

The Washington Coastline

Washington has miles and miles of salt-water shore: sandy Pacific Ocean beaches to the south, the wild rocky coast to the north, and Puget Sound, that inland sea reaching for about 100 miles into the heart of western Washington. Much of the coastline remains virgin wilderness, but access to the beach in some locations is limited by the rapid development of resort towns, real estate developments, and private land owners. In addition, a number of Indian Reservations border the sea-coast.

Puget Sound and The San Juan Islands

Officially Puget Sound includes the areas between the entrance to Hood Canal and the southern tip of the Sound, but in popular usage it includes most of the inland sea to the north, and the San Juan Islands. Puget Sound is an enormous glacially carved scar on the earth's surface. Typically in this region the bottom drops off abruptly a short distance from shore and the narrow sand, gravel, or cobblestone beaches are frequently below sand and gravel bluffs. The area provides an extensive habitat for bay clams, such as Horse Clams, Butters, Little-necks, Heart Cockles, and Geoducks. At the southern tip of the Sound numerous streams and rivers feed the broad tidal mud flats of Olympia and provide important feeding grounds for waterfowl. When visiting the port of Seattle walk along the busy waterfront: within a few blocks you will see fishing boats, enormous freighters and fire boats, and tempting open-air markets offering Dungeness Crab, halibut, clams, oysters, scallops, and octopus.

The 473 San Juan Islands and rocks are stepping stones along the arm of the sea that reaches northward from Puget Sound. Most of the islands are wooded and rocky; a few are settled, but many remain uninhabited. Swift tidal currents throughout the area contribute to a variety of shores: exposed sterile gravel beaches; rocky reefs and headlands; protected bays of mixed sand, mud, and cobblestone; and the occasional sandy beach. At low tide a protected rocky shore exposes long-spined red urchins, bright sea cucumbers, and the usual collection of sea stars, crabs, and snails and offshore kelp forests.

The Straits of Juan de Fuca

The Straits of Juan de Fuca provide the connecting channel between the Pacific Ocean and Puget Sound. The coastline is generally steep, with narrow beaches of coarse sand or boulders, and frequent hard sedimentary outcroppings embedded with fossil clams and snails. Unfortunately much of the coastline is privately owned, making access to the water difficult. Dungeness Spit, a long arm of sand jutting into the Straits, is famous for its Dungeness Crab; a lighthouse warns of shallow waters. Cape Flattery lies at the tip of the peninsula where untamed breakers carve great caverns and blowholes in the cliffs, and where marine life abounds. At the south end of the beach, Point of Arches, with its offshore stacks and needles, sea caves and arches, forms a spectacular barrier to walking any farther on the beach.

The Washington Coastline

The Northwest Coast

The spectacular "Olympic Strip" of the Olympic National Park is in places as narrow as a half mile, but extends miles along the seacoast. Because it has very few roads it is a favorite hike for wilderness backpackers, often the best trail being the beach itself. A tide table is necessary if you wish to pass by headlands in minutes at low tide; the trip overland through dense bush may take hours. Everywhere the Olympic rain forest creeps down to the sea — delicate ferns carpet the floor; dense bushes of salal tower overhead; and goat's beard and mosses drape Douglas fir and Red Cedar. Cape Alava at the northern end of the coast trail is generally shrouded by a thick blanket of fog. Walk five miles farther to the south end of Point of Arches and to nearby Carson Sea Cave, a spectacular "garden" of intertidal plants and animals. The small salmon harbor of La Push, in the Quillayute Indian Reservation, and rugged Teahwhit Head have some of the most scenic areas on the coast — white sandy beaches, seastacks, and tidepools lined with brightly colored sea stars, urchins, and anemones. An easier trail leads in a southerly direction to Toleak Point; two of the three headlands can be crossed at low tide, the three can be climbed on trails at high tide. Kalaloch has clean sandy beaches with excellent Razor Clam digging, surf fishing, and beach combing. From Ruby Beach to Queets the road runs close to the shore, but beach access is limited to three small towns in between. The beaches of the Indian village of Tahalah on the Quinalt Indian Reservation are closed to the general public.

The Southwest Coast

The southwest coast extends from Moclips to the Columbia River. Almost the entire shoreline is composed of fine sandy beaches interrupted occasionally by rocky bluffs, and wherever Razor Clams dig rapidly at the surf line there is a resort town with tourist facilities. The smallest is Moclips; each succeeding town to the south is larger. During the summer armies of clam diggers and surf fishermen invade the productive beaches, but in winter only seasoned beach combers venture out to collect prize pieces of driftwood, Japanese fishing floats, sand dollars, and empty snail shells. The drive around Willapa Bay reveals broad, flat, swampy ground, bogs, and mud flats, facts that make the Willapa National Wildlife Refuge an important sanctuary for a wide variety of shorebirds. The mud flats also make productive oyster farms a possibility. Beyond Oysterville, Leadbetter State Park occupies the northerly tip of the peninsula, a harsh wind-swept desert of sand dunes, grasses, and shrubs — a bird sanctuary protecting some two hundred species.

Officially designated "North Beach Peninsula" but more popularly known as "Long Beach", the twenty-eight miles of long flat sandy beaches on Washington's exposed southwest shore provide some of the state's most popular vacation spots. The long expanse of sand comes suddenly to an end at North Head, a rocky headland south of Seaview. A glance back up the peninsula from the lighthouse on the bluffs reveals white arching breakers marching along the long ribbon of sandy beaches backed by low grassy dunes. From the Cape Disappointment Lighthouse watch the ocean waves fight the currents of the Columbia River.

The Washington Coastline

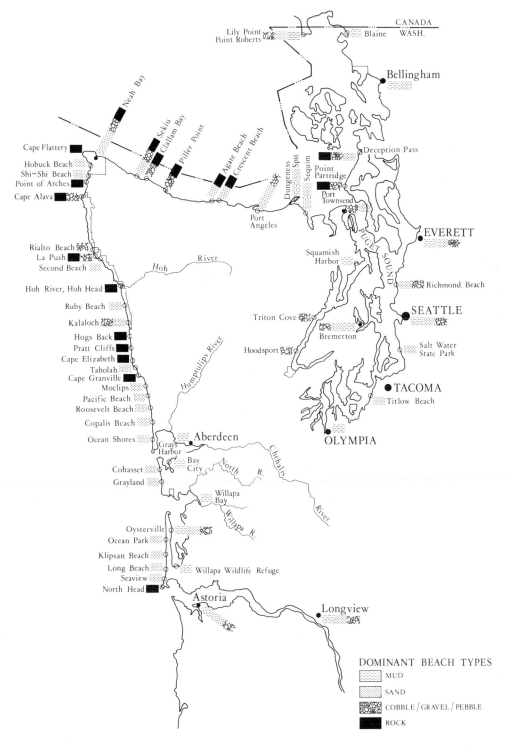

CANADA
WASH.

Lily Point
Point Roberts
Blaine

● Bellingham

Neah Bay

Sekiu
Clallam Bay
Piller Point
Agate Beach
Crescent Beach

Deception Pass

Cape Flattery
Hobuck Beach
Shi–Shi Beach
Point of Arches
Cape Alava

Dungeness Spit
Sequim
Point Partridge
Port Townsend

Port Angeles

● EVERETT

Rialto Beach
La Push
Second Beach

Hoh River, Hoh Head

Squamish Harbor

Richmond Beach

Ruby Beach
Kalaloch
Hogs Back
Pratt Cliffs
Cape Elizabeth
Taholah
Cape Granville
Moclips
Pacific Beach
Roosevelt Beach
Copalis Beach
Ocean Shores

● SEATTLE

Triton Cove

Bremerton

Hoodsport

Salt Water
State Park

Aberdeen
Grays Harbor
Cohasset
Bay City
Grayland

North R.

Chehalis River

● TACOMA
Titlow Beach

OLYMPIA

Willapa Bay

Oysterville
Ocean Park
Klipsan Beach
Long Beach
Seaview
North Head

Willapa R.

Willapa Wildlife Refuge

Astoria

● Longview

PUGET SOUND

Hoh River

Humptulips River

DOMINANT BEACH TYPES

MUD

SAND

COBBLE / GRAVEL / PEBBLE

ROCK

217

The British Columbia Coastline

British Columbia has 16,900 miles of coastline! Islands, headlands, inlets, reefs, and bays! And most of them inaccessible except by boat.

But this is not a seacoast in constant struggle with the elements; it is, in fact, except for the west coast of Vancouver Island and the Queen Charlottes, almost wholly protected.

Vancouver Island

Between Victoria on the south end of Vancouver Island and Campbell River on the east side lies a protected coast, a gentle sort of shoreline. Some of the sandy beaches, such as those at Parksville and Qualicum, stretch out for over a mile when the tide goes out. Miracle Beach Park has a mixture of magnificent sand and cobblestone, the habitat of bay clams. Campbell River offers a variety of marine activities: fishing, clamming, oyster growing, and crabbing.

North from Campbell River stretches a formidable and continuous chain of fiords — steep rocky mountains rising right out of the sea, and trees and dense undergrowth crowding to the water's edge. Kelsey Bay, Port McNeil and Port Hardy, on coastal plains but forced to withstand storms blowing down from Alaska, have a variety of beaches, mud, sand, and rock. This is a transitional region which supports a great assortment of intertidal plants and animals; a wild land, calm at one moment, surf-swept the next.

At the top end of the island lies Cape Scott: here the Pacific breakers roll without interruption, battering themselves to white froth against rocky headlands and wide expanses of clean, white sandy beaches. South of Cape Scott, the western seacoast becomes a mix of wild beaches, rocky headlands, and inlets which go deep into rugged mountains and forests. Everywhere evidence of violent action — broken rocks, sea caves, needles, hay stacks, wind sculptured trees. And strung between the headlands are the beaches. The finest is Long Beach — a magnificent twelve-mile stretch of clean, white sand where at low tide Razor Claims dig rapidly. At the entrance to Barkley Sound, at the Broken Group Islands, squads of Killer Whales and Gray Whales cruise by, and sea lions and seals haul themselves out onto rocky shores.

The southwest coast, between Cape Beale and Sooke, is a place of waterfalls, sandstone cliffs, sea caves, and sandy beaches. The unique rock formations at Botany Bay, near Port Renfrew, are cut out of sandstone and blackish shale; a halfmoon arena overlooks beautifully shaped tidepools, caves, and surge channels — a prolific "marine garden" of intertidal life: Sea Palms, urchins, anemones, sea stars, goose barnacles, chitons, snails, crabs, and corraline algae. At Bamfield the Marine Research Station has access to some of the most productive intertidal sea life on the Pacific coast. Between Port Renfrew and Victoria, East Sooke Park is a large semi-wilderness with twisting, and often difficult, trails. A dropping tide reveals beaches of rock, pebbles, and sand.

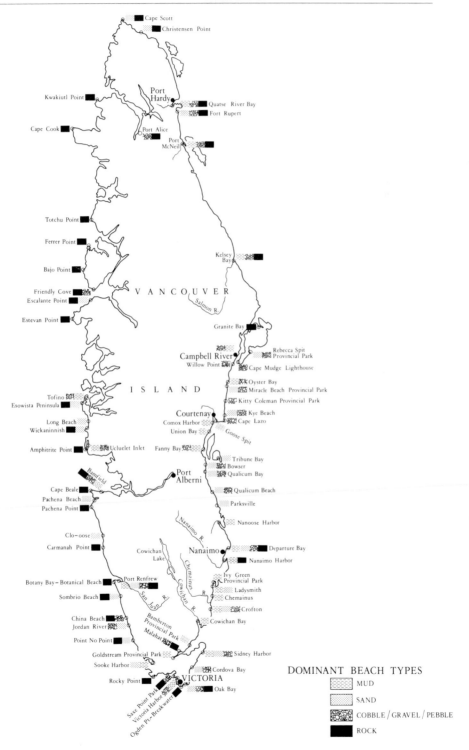

Cape Scott
Christensen Point

Kwakiutl Point

Port Hardy
Quatse River Bay
Fort Rupert

Cape Cook

Port Alice
Port McNeil

Totchu Point

Ferrer Point

Bajo Point

Friendly Cove
Escalante Point

Estevan Point

V A N C O U V E R

Salmon R.

Kelsey Bay

Granite Bay

Rebecca Spit Provincial Park

Campbell River
Willow Point
Cape Mudge Lighthouse

I S L A N D

Oyster Bay
Miracle Beach Provincial Park
Kitty Coleman Provincial Park

Tofino
Esowista Peninsula

Courtenay
Comox Harbor
Union Bay

Kye Beach
Cape Lazo

Goose Spit

Long Beach
Wickaninnish

Amphitrite Point
Ucluelet Inlet
Fanny Bay

Tribune Bay
Bowser
Qualicum Bay

Bamfield

Port Alberni

Qualicum Beach

Cape Beale
Pachena Beach
Pachena Point

Parksville

Nanaimo R.

Nanoose Harbor

Clo-oose
Carmanah Point

Cowichan Lake

Nanaimo
Departure Bay
Nanaimo Harbor

Botany Bay – Botanical Beach
Sombrio Beach

Port Renfrew

San Juan R.

Chemainus R.

Cowichan R.

Ivy Green Provincial Park
Ladysmith
Chemainus
Crofton

China Beach
Jordan River
Point No Point

Bamberton Provincial Park
Malahat

Cowichan Bay

Goldstream Provincial Park
Sooke Harbor

Sidney Harbor

Cordova Bay

Rocky Point

VICTORIA

Oak Bay

Saxe Point Park
Victoria Harbor
Ogden Pt – Breakwater

DOMINANT BEACH TYPES

MUD

SAND

COBBLE / GRAVEL / PEBBLE

ROCK

The British Columbia Coastline

The Islands of the Strait of Georgia

Off the southeast coast of Vancouver Island, between Victoria and Nanaimo, lie the Gulf Islands, some twenty-six major islands and numerous islets and reefs. Much of the waterfront acreage is private, but there are several public access points. Most of the coastline is rocky, often plunging abruptly to the ocean. In many places sandstone headlands have been carved by water and weather into fantastic shapes, a particularly beautiful example being the seacliffs at Malaspina Galleries on Gabriola Island. In bays and the protected sides of spits, there are beaches of varying width and composition.

The more northerly islands of the Strait, such as Quadra Island and its nearby neighbor Cortes Island, are secluded places with spectacular beach scenery: white-capped mountain peaks suspended in the distant clouds, bald eagles perched atop weathered Douglas fir trees and, from May to September, pods of killer whales cruising briskly offshore. In some locations underwater mountain peaks cause the waters to boil. Rocky Mitlenatch Island is a nature park and a bird sanctuary with a resident naturalist. North of Quadra the islands are sparsely inhabited, if at all.

The British Columbia Mainland Coast

The international boundary between Canada and the United States of America passes through Boundary Bay, a broad tidal flat of sand and mud which dries out at low tide. Point Roberts lies at the tip of a promontory extending from the Fraser River delta south across the U.S. border. The point terminates in a low shingle shelf known as Lily Point where an enormous sandstone cliff towers above a beach of mixed sand, mud, and boulder. During extreme low tides a cobblestone reef comes into view. On the other side of the Bay, the protected sand beach of White Rock supports scattered eelgrass beds.

In the heart of the sprawling city of Vancouver, the thousand acre Stanley Park includes public beaches and virgin forest, the sea wall providing a view of sandy beaches, rocky outcrops, and seaweed covered boulders. Located in the park the Vancouver Public Aquarium displays a variety of marine animals. Within a few minutes drive of Stanley Park it is possible to explore Deep Cove, Cates Park, Wreck Beach, Spanish Banks, English Bay, Jericho Beach, and the Port Moody mud flats.

Lighthouse Park, nine miles north west of Vancouver, combines the best of the forest and the sea. Rounded bare granite rocks drop abruptly to the water and reveal marine animals accustomed to heavy surf: the location of the park at Point Atkinson exposes it to the heavy seas. Only five miles farther, Whytecliff Park provides hiking trails, a small playground, and a protected cobblestone beach. From Horseshoe Bay, around the point, the government ferries leave for Vancouver Island and the Sechelt Peninsula.

Gibson's, two miles across the sound from Horseshoe Bay, is the first of several quiet seaside communities that dot the profile of the Sechelt, affectionately known as "The Sunshine Coast". The innumerable beaches of cobblestone, boulders, rocky outcroppings, and multi-colored pebbly-sand, support a large population of bay clams and oysters. North of Sechelt the villages thin out noticeably, and going to Powell River necessitates taking a second ferry across Jervis Inlet.

North of Powell River, Bella Coola, Bella Bella, Ocean Falls, Kitimat, and Prince Rupert are located where they are because of the commercial activity. The trip up the inlets offers little else but steep sided rocky fiords and frequent small beaches of mixed cobble, sand, and gravel. But at the heads of inlets, the variety of beach types offer endless exploratory possibilities, rocky shores, cobblestone beaches, mixed sand and mud beaches, and broad tidal mud flats.

Queen Charlotte Islands

Fifty miles offshore are more than one hundred and fifty islands grouped in a rough triangular shape and known as the Queen Charlottes. Wind, fog, and rain nourish the land. Naikoon Provincial Park occupies the northeast corner with its low flat shore of long sandy beach, graying drift logs, and dunes of shifting sand. The exposed surf-swept west coast alternates with black volcanic rocky reefs, long arching stretches of golden sand, and polished gravel beaches glittering with multi-colored agates. Leaning totem poles and Indian middens tell of how the Haidas harvested the good life: seaweeds, edible mussels, Razor Clams, bay clams, Dungeness Crab, halibut, salmon, seals, and Killer Whales.

Most of the mainland coast is inaccessible by road, but yachts, freighter-passenger ships, cruise ships, commercial fishing boats, and private pleasure craft go up and down the Inside Passage, that narrow corridor between the mainland and Vancouver Island and the Charlottes. Seen from ships the mainland coast is a continuous line of solid granite and volcanic mountains, with immense rivers of shimmering ice in the distance. All the way from Vancouver to Alaska little else but rocks and cliffs meet the sea; sandy beaches are small, and few and far between. Spectacular deep water fiords send long sinuous arms fifty to seventy miles into the land, their sides sometimes rising in unbroken slopes to 8,000 feet above sea level, the width varying from one half a mile to two miles. A ship plying the Inside Passage is in protected waters most of the way up the coast to about Prince Rupert. From that point north Pacific breakers roll untamed to crash against the granite cliffs of the exposed Alaskan outer coast.

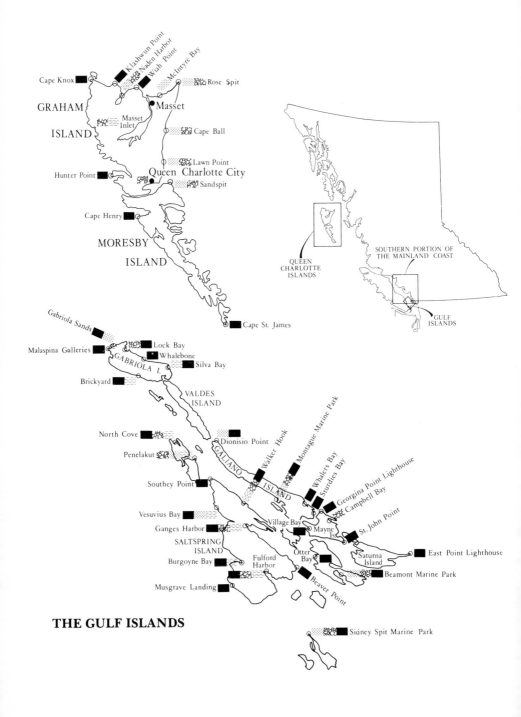

THE GULF ISLANDS

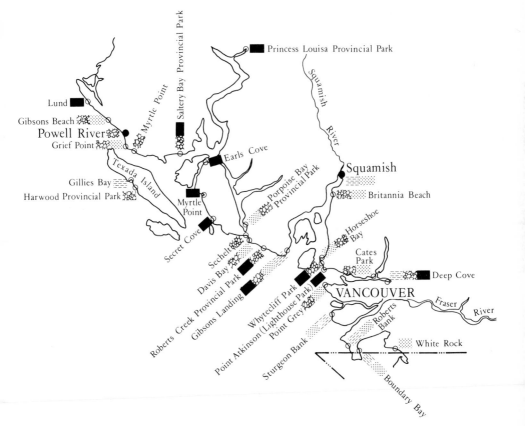

Princess Louisa Provincial Park

Squamish River

Saltery Bay Provincial Park

Lund

Gibsons Beach

Powell River

Grief Point

Myrtle Point

Earls Cove

Squamish

Texada Island

Gillies Bay

Harwood Provincial Park

Porpoise Bay Provincial Park

Britannia Beach

Myrtle Point

Secret Cove

Horseshoe Bay

Sechelt

Cates Park

Davis Bay

Roberts Creek Provincial Park

Gibsons Landing

Whytecliff Park

Point Atkinson (Lighthouse Park)

Point Grey

VANCOUVER

Deep Cove

Fraser River

Roberts Bank

Sturgeon Bank

White Rock

Boundary Bay

DOMINANT BEACH TYPES

MUD

SAND

COBBLE / GRAVEL / PEBBLE

ROCK

THE SOUTHERN PORTION OF THE MAINLAND COAST

Clothing And Equipment

Proper clothing is very important for any trip to the seashore. Our west coast weather conditions are extremely unpredictable: sun, wind, rain, hail, and snow possible on the same day. Over dress rather than under dress.

On hot sunny days, reflections off the water can cause severe sunburns and even sunstroke, particularly for individuals not frequently out-of-doors. On first trips always wear a long-sleeved cotton shirt as protection from the sun, and during poor weather wear the shirt under wool or under rain gear.

Keep dry. A variety of synthetics may be worn, but windbreakers, sweat shirts, and cotton jackets are not substitutes for the water-proof rain gear worn by fishermen. Wear good thick-soled rubber boots, woolen socks, a long nylon or rubberized rain coat with a hood, or a fisherman's rain coat with rubberized pants.

Cold weather needn't ruin trips to the seashore, but wear wool. Wool, even when wet, retains body warmth more than any other material. On cold days wear a heavy woolen sweater, woolen mittens, a woolen hat that covers the ears, and long woolen or thermal underwear.

It is quite possible, in fact maybe even desirable, to make several trips to the seashore without packing along any equipment. But once familiar with the more obvious plants and animals, choose a few pieces of equipment to help you discover a richer variety and a greater number of organisms. Place an animal in a clear plastic bag or plastic bucket half-filled with sea water to have a better understanding of how the animal behaves when the tide is high.

Suggested Equipment:

- binoculars
- clear plastic freezer bags
- clear plastic jars
- face mask
- kitchen sieve or small net
- magnifying glass
- note pad and pencil
- plastic pail
- putty knife or pocket knife
- shovel with short handle

118 Keeping warm and dry

Each region of the world has its own tide tables, most of them drawn up on a 24:00 hour clock. Acquire a tide table for the appropriate area of Oregon, Washington, and British Columbia from any boat marina or large book store. Pretend for a moment that you want to take a trip to the seashore on Saturday, May 25, 1978.

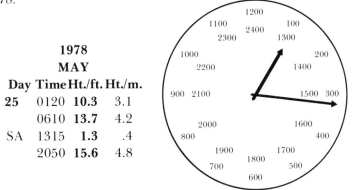

1978

MAY

Day	Time	Ht./ft.	Ht./m.
25	0120	**10.3**	3.1
	0610	**13.7**	4.2
SA	1315	**1.3**	.4
	2050	**15.6**	4.8

On the tide table above, the highest tide of 4.8 meters (15.6 feet) occurs at 2050 (8:50 p.m.) and the lowest of .4 meters (1.3 feet) at 1315 (1:15 p.m.)

On the west coast the best tides for observing seashores occurs during the daytime in the spring and summer months. The fall and winter have high tides during the day and low tides at night. The ideal tide level for studying intertidal plants and animals is .9 meters (3 feet) or less on Vancouver B.C. tide tables, and 2.1 meters (6.8 feet) or less on Puget Sound tide tables. Because Canadian and U.S. tide tables are not based on the same system you must have a local tide table.

Do not, however, rule out fall and winter. Consider mid-tide or high tide, too. Start the day a little earlier. Visit the beach at night with flashlights — a thrilling adventure because many intertidal animals which are inactive during the day search for food at night.

Illustrated Glossary of Terms

Abalone. A large snail valued both for food and for its single flattened shell lined with mother-of-pearl.

Abdomen. The last part of the body: head, thorax, abdomen.

Adaptation. The changing of structure or form or habitats of a plant or animal to improve its chances of survival in a particular place.

Aeolid. A type of nudibranch covered with finger-like gills.

Alga. One of the more primitive plant forms able to use the sun's energy for making food: ocean seaweed.

Amphipod. Tiny crustaceans, about 5 to 10 mm in length, with short antennae and flattened bodies feeding on detritus, and themselves the food of countless marine animals.

Antenna. A "feeler" or pair of "feelers" on the heads of insects, shrimps, and crabs.

Anus. The opening of the digestive tract at the rear end of an animal.

Apex. The tip of the shell of a univalve such as snails, limpets, or barnacles.

Appendage. An arm or other limb or projection that branches from an animal's body: e.g. crabs' legs, shrimp antennae.

Bacteria. (pl) Any of numerous widely distributed one-celled micro-organisms having both plant and animal characteristics.

Barnacle. Any of several species of small sea animals with a thin, cone-shaped shell. The larvae cement themselves permanently to rocks, wharves, and the bottoms of ships.

Bivalve. A shellfish having two shells hinged together by a muscle: oysters, clams, cockles, scallops, and mussels.

Bladelet. The small flat blades protruding just above the holdfast of some seaweeds.

Brachiopod. A group of bivalves with a flexible stem which attaches the animal to rocks.

Bryozoan. Any of a phylum of animals living together in colonies which form thin crusty patches on rocks and seaweeds.

Byssus threads. Strong threads produced by a gland and attaching mussels and some clams and oysters to rocks and other hard surfaces.

Calcium. A hard chemical element common in limestone, teeth, and shells.

Camouflage. A color pattern enabling some animals to hide in, or blend in with, their surroundings.

Carapace. The hard shell covering the body and backs of crabs and shrimps.

Carnivore. An animal feeding on the flesh of other animals.

Cerata. Fleshy spike-like projections on the upper surface of some nudibranchs, which take the place of gills.

Chiton. Any of several species of primitive sea animals having a body made up of eight separate plates, a girdle that may be scaly or bristly, and a large, flat muscular foot which allows the animal to adhere tightly to rocks.

Cirrus. (pl. cirri) A soft flexible appendage for straining plankton from water, as in barnacles.

Clam. Any of a group of bivalves with siphons to draw in and out for eating, a large mantle cavity, a hatchet-shaped foot for digging, and living partly or wholly buried in sand, mud, or gravel.

Colony. A group of plants and animals of the same kind growing or living together: bryozoans, corals, hydroids, sponges, and jellyfishes.

Column. The main body or stem of a sea anemone.

Commensalism. A relationship between two kinds of organisms in which one, the commensal, obtains food or other benefits from the second, the host, without damage to either. Scaleworms live commensally with limpets, chitons, and sea stars.

Community. A group of plants and animals living in the same area and depending on one another for survival.

Coral. A lower animal that builds a limy skeleton.

Coralline Alga. A group of strange looking algae made up of calcium, usually reddish-pink or purplish-pink, and generally quite brittle.

Crab. A crustacean having a flattened body, four pairs of legs, a pair of grasping claws, and a small abdomen.

Crustacean. An animal with a hard outside shell, antennae, mandibles, and compound eyes, and living in water: lobsters, crabs, shrimps, amphipods, and barnacles.

Detritus. Decaying plants and animals.

Diatom. Any one-celled microscopic plant living in water, some forming a major component of plankton and others contributing to the thin brown scum that falls to the bottom.

Dorid. A type of nudibranch with a flattened, plump body, a rough surface, and branched gills located in a ring on the back.

Dorsal. On or in the direction of the topside or back of an animal.

Estuary. The wide mouth of a river that flows into the sea and into which the tide flows.

Feces. Solid waste material passed out from the body through the anus.

Filter feeder. An animal equipped with hairs, tentacles, sieves, or other devices for straining plankton and minute particles of detritus and diatoms from the water: clams, oysters, scallops, mussels, and barnacles.

Flank. The sides of an animal's body; in birds, below or under the closed wings.

Frond. The blade-like or leaf-like expansion of seaweeds in which the function of stem and leaf are not distinguished.

Foot. The wide flat-ended or wedge-shaped muscle used for crawling or digging: snails, limpets, chitons, abalones, and clams.

Genus. A term in classification of plants and animals; a group of related species; the first listed and capitalized name of a double scientific name e.g., Homo sapiens.

Gill. An organ used for underwater breathing by fishes, gilled worms, snails, limpets, and nudibranchs.

Girdle. A tough band at the edge of the plates of a chiton, often decorated with short bristles or scales.

Habitat. The place in which a plant or animal lives.

Herbivore. An animal feeding on plants: limpets, chitons, and many snails.

Hinge. A spring-like structure joining together the two shells of a bivalve.

Holdfast. A structure anchoring seaweeds to rocks and other hard surfaces.

Host. An organism providing a home in or on itself, or in its burrow, for another.

Hydroid. A primitive colonial animal with tentacles and stinging cells; related to sea anemones.

Intertidal. The area between the high tide mark and the low tide mark on a seashore.

Illustrated Glossary of Terms

Isopod. An animal with a long, flattened body, usually quite small, and having seven pairs of short legs of about equal size.

Jellyfish. A jellylike, free-swimming sea animal with a bell-shaped, partly transparent body, and generally with long stinging threads on the surface.

Kelp. Large, strap-like, brown seaweeds with strong holdfasts.

Larva. (larvae pl.) The free-swimming stage in the development of an animal after birth: egg, larva, adult; or, egg, larva, pupa, adult.

Limpet. A slow-moving animal having a large, flat muscular foot and a hard shell into which the animal can partially withdraw.

Madreporite. See sieve plate.

Mandibles. The first pair of many mouth parts or jaws for manipulating foods: crabs, lobsters, shrimps.

Mantle. An outer sheet of fleshy tissue secreting the shell and forming a chamber to enclose the internal organs: in shellfish, snails, limpets, and chitons, or, the back, shoulders, and closed wings of a bird.

Molt. To shed the hard, protective outer covering; the covering left behind after an organism, such as the shrimp, crab or barnacle, crawls out of it in order to grow.

Mussel. A bivalve clinging to rocks and pilings with byssus threads.

Nemertean. A long, unsegmented carnivorous worm with a long, extendible proboscis.

Nudibranch. A soft bodied slug-like snail with branched gills, without a shell, or at least without one large enough into which the animal can withdraw, and divided into two broad groups, the aeolids and dorids.

aeolid   *dorid*

Octopus. An animal having a bag-shaped body with eight more-or-less equal arms, and with suction cups on the underside of the arms for grasping prey.

Operculum. A trapdoor, used for closing the shell of a snail or the tube of a worm; a protective device for an animal that has withdrawn into its shell or tube.

Oral disc. The mouth-opening and ring of tentacles of a sea anemone.

Organism. A single living plant or animal.

Oyster. A type of shellfish characterized by an irregular, double shell.

Paralyze. To inject a toxin in order to make a prey inactive.

Pedal disc. The base of a sea anemone, the part which attaches the animal to rocks or other hard surfaces.

Phylum. In the classification of living organisms, a large group of obviously interrelated forms: e.g., sponges (Phylum Porifera).

Plankton. The minute plants and animals drifting or swimming in the ocean; the food of filter-feeders.

Polyp. An individual member of a hydroid or coral colony, or a sea anemone, or bryzoan.

Predator. An animal that eats other animals.

Prey. An animal eaten by another animal.

Proboscis. Specialized mouth parts that can be extended for sucking.

Radula. A rasping tongue-like structure used for scraping food from rocks and sometimes for boring through shells.

Ray. The arm of a sea star.

Regeneration. The ability to replace lost body parts, such as an arm or leg.

Reproduction. The process by which new members of a species are produced.

Rhinophores. A pair of elaborate tentacles on the upper surface of the head of nudibranchs.

Rib. On a shell: a raised line or ridge running up and down a shell.

Salinity. The amount of salt contained in water.

Sand Dollar. An animal having a very flattened, circular body covered with spines and showing the five-star pattern; related to sea stars, sea urchins, and sea cucumbers.

Scallop. A bivalve with a "scalloped" shell.

Scavenger. An animal that eats the remains and wastes of other animals and plants.

Sea Anemone. An attached marine animal with a body cavity broken up into a number of chambers, tentacles with stinging cells around the mouth opening, and having a flower-like appearance.

Sea Cucumber. An elongated animal with generally five rows of tube feet running the length of the body, and a ring of mop-like tentacles around the mouth.

Sea Pen. A plume-shaped, carnivorous animal having little tentacles located on the plume-like branches; related to sea anemones and jellyfish.

Sea Star. A star-shaped animal having a central body with five or more rays, and tube feet which adhere firmly to rocks and aid in movement.

Sea Squirt. A sea animal having a leathery covering, and contracting the body to squirt jets of water.

Sea Urchin. Animals with long, bristling spines, tube feet, and five moveable jaws; related to sea stars, sea urchins, and sand dollars.

Seaweed. A marine alga.

Segment. A section, division, or part of the body having a structure similar to other sections, divisions, or parts.

Shrimp. Any long-tailed crustacean having a fused head and thorax, and segmented abdomen.

Sieve plate. A perforated calcareous plate on the upper surface of sea stars and sea urchins permitting water to enter the water-vascular system.

Siphon. A tube-like structure in certain marine animals, such as clams and octopuses, allowing the passage of sea water.

Snail. A small, slow-moving animal with eyes sometimes on stalks, a muscular foot, and a hard coiled shell into which the snail can at least partially withdraw.

Illustrated Glossary of Terms

Species. (sp.) A particular kind of animal or plant able to breed with one another, but not so likely to breed with those of other species.

Specimen. An individual plant or animal.

Sponge. A group of colonial permanently attached animals having soft porous skeletons and being of various sizes, shapes, and colors.

Stipe. The stem-like part of many seaweeds.

Subspecies. (spp.) A subdivision of a species, a group immediately below a species whose members are capable of interbreeding successfully with those of other subspecies of the same species, but are separated by geographical barriers.

Swimmerettes. The abdominal or swimming legs of some crustaceans, such as lobsters and shrimp.

Tentacle. A long, arm-like appendage, generally used for feeding.

Test. The hard shells of a sea urchin, sea star, or sand dollar through which the spines project and the tube feet extend.

Thorax. In insects and many crustceans, between the head and abdomen, the middle part of the body.

Tube feet. Special attachment organs for movement and for collecting food: as in sea stars, cucumbers, and urchins.

Univalve. A shellfish with only one shell: snails, limpets, and abalones.

Valve. One of the two halves of a clam shell, or one of the plates covering a barnacle when it is withdrawn into its shell.

Ventral. The lower side of the body; opposite of dorsal.

Water-vascular system. A system of canals, bulbs, and tube feet filled with sea water: involved in locomotion of sea stars, and sea urchins, and sea cucumbers.

Whorl. A spiraling turn of a snail shell, the largest whorl being the body whorl containing most of the snail's body.

Zonation. An arrangement of plants and animals in horizontal layers on the shore.

General Books About Seashore Plants And Animals

Amos, William H.　　*The life of the seashore.* New York: McGraw-Hill Book Company, 1966.

Barnes, Robert D.　　*Invertebrate zoology.* Philadelphia: Sanders Company, 1963.

Burton, R.　　*The seashore and its wildlife.* London: Orbis Publishing, 1977.

Carefoot, Tom.　　*Pacific seashores.* Vancouver: J.J. Douglas, 1977.

Carl, G. Clifford.　　*Guide to marine life of British Columbia.* Handbook No. 21, Victoria: British Columbia Provincial Museum, 1966.

Carson, Rachel.　　*The edge of the sea.* New York: Mentor and Plume Books, 1955.

Cornwall, I.E.　　*The barnacles of British Columbia.* Handbook No. 7, Victoria: British Columbia Provincial Museum, 1970.

Fairbanks, F. and C. Flora.　　*The sound and the sea.* Third Edition. Washington: The Washington State Department of Printing, 1977.

Furlong, Marjorie and Virginia Pill.　　*Starfish: Guides to identification and methods of preserving.* Washington: Ellison Industries, 1970.

Griffith, Lela M.　　*The intertidal univalves of British Columbia.* Handbook No. 26, Victoria: British Columbia Provincial Museum, 1967.

Hewlett, Stefani and Gilbey.　　*Sea life of the Pacific Northwest.* Toronto: McGraw-Hill Ryerson Ltd., 1976.

Johnson, Myrtle E. and Harry Snook.　　*Seashore animals of the Pacific Coast.* Toronto: General Publishing Company, 1967.

Keen, Myra and Eugene Coan.　　*Marine molluscan genera of Western North America: An illustrated key.* Second Edition. Stanford: California University Press, 1974.

Kozloff, Eugene N.　　*Seashore life of Puget Sound, the Strait of Georgia, and the San Juan Archipelago.* Seattle: University of Washington Press, 1973.

Quayle, D.B. and N. Bourne.　　*The clam fisheries of British Columbia.* Bulletin No. 179. Ottawa: Fisheries Research Board of Canada, 1972.

Quayle, D.B.　　*The intertidal bivalves of British Columbia.* Handbook No. 27. Victoria: British Columbia Provincial Museum, 1973.

Bibliography

Rice, Tom — *Marine shells of the Pacific Coast.* Tacoma: ERCO, Inc., 1973.

Ricketts, Edward R. and Jack Calvin. — *Between Pacific tides.* Fourth Edition, revised. Stanford: Stanford University Press, 1968.

Smith, Lynwood. — *Living shores of the Pacific Northwest.* Seattle: Pacific Search, 1976.

Smith, Ralph and James Carlton. — *Light's manual: Intertidal invertebrates of the Central California Coast.* Third Edition, revised. Berkeley: University of California, 1974.

Somerton, David and Craig Murray. — *Field guide to the fish of Puget Sound and the Northwest Coast.* A Washington Sea Grant Publication. Seattle: University of Washington Press, 1976.

Stephenson, T.A. — *Life between tidemarks on rocky shores.* San Francisco: W.H. Freeman & Company, 1972.

Vancouver Natural History Society. — *Nature west coast: As seen in Lighthouse Park.* Vancouver: Discovery Press, 1973.

White, James. — *Seashells of the Pacific Northwest.* Portland: Binford & Mort, 1976.

Zottoli, Robert. — *Introduction to marine environments.* Saint Louis: The C.V. Mosby Company, 1972.

Books About Seaweed

Dawson, E.Y. — *How to know the seaweeds.* Iowa: W.M.C. Brown, 1956.

Guberlet, Muriel Lewin. — *Seaweeds at ebb tide.* Seattle: University of Washington Press, 1962.

Scagel, Robert F. — *Guide to common seaweeds of British Columbia.* Handbook No. 27, Victoria: British Columbia Provincial Museum, 1967.

Waaland, Robert. — *Common seaweeds of the Pacific Coast.* Vancouver: Pacific Search, 1977.

Books About Shorebirds

Gabrielson, Ira and Stanley Jewett.	*Birds of the Pacific Northwest*. Portland: Dover Publications, 1970.
Guiguet, C.J.	*The birds of British Columbia: Handbook No. 13, gulls, terns, jaegers, and skua*. Victoria: British Columbia Provincial Museum, 1972.
Guiguet, C.J.	*The birds of British Columbia: Handbook No. 15, waterfowl*. Victoria: British Columbia Provincial Museum, 1973.
Guiguet, C.J.	*The birds of British Columbia: Handbook No. 29, diving birds and tube-nosed swimmers*. Victoria: British Columbia Provincial Museum, 1971.
Godfrey, W. Earl.	*The birds of Canada*. Bulletin No. 203. Ottawa: National Museum of Canada, 1966.
Kortright, F.H.	*The ducks, geese and swans of North America*. Washington, D.C.: Wildlife Management Institute, 1942.
Nehls, Harry B.	*Familiar birds of Northwest shores and waters*. Sponsored by Portland Audubon Society, Portland: Durham & Downey, Inc., 1975.
Peterson, Roger Tory.	*A field guide to western birds*. Sponsored by National Audubon Society. Boston: Houghton Mifflin Company, 1969.
Rodgers, John.	*Shorebirds and predators, birds of the Pacific Northwest*. Volume 1. Vancouver: J.J. Douglas, 1974.
Taverner, P.A.	*Birds of Western Canada*. Museum Bulletin No. 41, Biological Series. Ottawa: Department of Mines, 1926.
Udvardy, Miklos D.	*The Audubon Society field guide to North American Birds: Western Region*. New York: Knopf, 1977.
Wetmore, Alexander.	*Water, prey, and game birds of North America*. Sponsored by National Geographic Society. Washington, D.C.: National Geographic Society, 1965.

Books About Seashore Plants

Haskin, Leslie.	*Wild flowers of the Pacific Coast*. Portland: Binford & Mort, 1970.
Munz, Philip A.	*Shore wildflowers of California, Oregon, and Washington*. Berkeley: University of California Press, 1973.
Wiedemann, A. La Rea Dennis, and Frank Smith.	*Plants of the Oregon Coastal Dunes*. Corvallis: Oregon State University Press, 1974.

Index to Pages

Index to Pages

235

Index to Pages

Index to Pages

Index to Pages

Index to Pages